Donald Phillip Verene

The Science of Cookery and the Art of Eating Well

Philosophical and Historical Reflections on Food and Dining in Culture

STUDIES IN MEDICAL PHILOSOPHY

Edited by Alexander Gungov and Friedrich Luft

ISSN 2367-4377

Donald Phillip Verene

THE SCIENCE OF COOKERY AND THE ART OF EATING WELL

Philosophical and Historical Reflections on Food and Dining in Culture

ibidem-Verlag
Stuttgart

Bibliographic information published by the Deutsche Nationalbibliothek
Die Deutsche Nationalbibliothek lists this publication in the Deutsche Nationalbibliografie;
detailed bibliographic data are available in the Internet at http://dnb.d-nb.de.

Bibliografische Information der Deutschen Nationalbibliothek
Die Deutsche Nationalbibliothek verzeichnet diese Publikation in der Deutschen
Nationalbibliografie; detaillierte bibliografische Daten sind im Internet über http://dnb.d-nb.de
abrufbar.

ISSN: 2367-4377

ISBN-13: 978-3-8382-1198-5

© *ibidem*-Verlag / *ibidem* Press

Stuttgart, Germany 2018

In memory of

Eleanor Grant Verene

whose recipes first formed my culinary world

A tavola non s'invecchia.

At table one does not grow old.

Contents

Preface

In the second chapter of Ecclesiastes, the wisdom of Solomon is: "There is nothing better for mortals than to eat and drink, and find enjoyment in their toil." Two things distinctive to human culture are the development of language and the cooking of food. These two abilities come together in the art of dining. The meal unites food and conversation. The pleasures of the table and of table-talk go back as far as the poems of Homer.

The science of cookery and the art of eating well are not medicine, but they are allied with medicine from its earliest conception. Galen, in discussing the importance of nutrition in the *Method of Medicine*, says: "In short, the chief point of nourishment is to let it be easily digested and nutritious" (7.6). Medicine is directly concerned with the prevention and healing of disease. In its broader sense, it is concerned with the well-being of human beings. In this concern, cooking and eating well play a role. Proper nutrition is essential to the health of the body and the conviviality of the meal and the institution of dining is of great value for promoting the tranquility of the psyche.

The theme of this book is the importance of home cooking and how it depends upon and maintains tradition. The art of eating well is enhanced by a knowledge of ingredients and an awareness of the history of dining. Such knowledge gives context to the daily event of the meal, an event that is present in every culture and as old as culture itself. The art of dining, like the art of living of which it is a part, is a way to order the self and its place in the world.

Chapter 1 is a general view of cooking and dining, as begun by the ancient Greeks and Romans, and progressing to the famous text of Brillat-Savarin, *The Physiology of Taste*. Chapter 2 is an interpretation of Plutarch's *Dinner of the Seven Wise Men*, his imaginative account of the gathering at

Delphi of the Seven Sages of Greece, at a dinner hosted by Periander, ruler of Corinth, whose conversation encompasses the nature of good government and the nature of the human soul. Chapter 3 is a condensation of the fifteen books of Athenaeus's treatise on the *Learned Banqueters* or *Deipnosophists*, a work which cites many other works, and which is itself frequently cited but rarely read. Chapter 4 discusses the two most famous cookbooks in Western culture: the Roman work of Apicius and the Florentine book of Artusi. Added to these are comments on some contemporary cookbooks, notably those of Giuliano Bugialli.

The theme of this book derives from my experience with and attachment to Italian cooking, acquired while living for extended periods in Florence over the past several decades. To shop at the Mercato Centrale at San Lorenzo is to confront a world of ingredients necessary to the Florentine table. When combined with the friendly conversations with its vendors, concerning the preparation of their wares, such shopping is a culinary education that no cookbook can supply. In Florentine cooking, as in Italian cooking generally, the quality of the ingredients, including their freshness, is the master key to the art of eating well.

It is only human to desire to eat well. But I find a more specific reason in the words of the great poet of the American language, author of the epic poem *The People, Yes*, Carl Sandburg, who was born and raised in the midwestern town of Galesburg, Illinois—as was I. Sandburg was asked what he wanted out of life. He replied, "Three things, maybe four: to be out of jail, to eat regular, to get what I write printed. And a little love at home and a little outside." The fourth was his way of expressing his wish to receive some recognition for his work, but he knew what every writer knows—that the recognition may not come. That's why it's important to eat regular.

Once again, I thank Molly Black Verene for her necessary and generous assistance in the preparation of the text.

Chapter 1

Introduction:
The Science of Cookery and the
Art of Eating Well

> Not only does cooking mark the
> transition from nature to culture,
> but through it and by means of it,
> the human state can be defined with
> all its attributes, even those that,
> like mortality, might seem to be the
> most unquestionably natural.
>
> Claude Lévi-Strauss
> *The Raw and the Cooked*

The First Meals

In the *Protagoras*, Plato relates the story of Prometheus and the acquisition of fire by humans (320d–22d).[1] There was a time when the gods existed but mortal beings did not. At the proper moment in the genesis of things, the gods molded the various forms of these beings inside the earth. They did this by blending earth and fire and various compounds. When the gods were ready to bring these beings into the world they put Prometheus and his brother Epimetheus in charge of assigning to each type its particular powers and abilities.

Epimetheus begged Prometheus to grant him the privilege of distributing these powers and abilities to the various species, and the agreement was made that, once the distribution was complete, Prometheus could inspect it. Thus allowed, Epimetheus supplied some with strength;

those that were weaker he made quick. To some he assigned wings and to others the means to burrow underground. For protection against the weather he gave some thick pelts and hides. He shod some with hooves and gave others claws. He also provided them with various forms of nourishment. Each species was equipped with what was needed for its survival.

When Epimetheus (whose name means "he who learns only from the event, the heedless") was finished, Prometheus (whose name means "he who knows in advance, who provides"), saw that all the available powers and abilities had been used up on the nonreasoning animals. The human race had been left entirely unequipped—naked, unshod, and unarmed—and it was already the day that all the animals, including the humans, were to be released from inside the earth into the light.

Prometheus, in order to provide the humans with some means of survival, stole fire for them from Hephaestus, the divine smith and master of the forge on Lemmos; from Athena he stole wisdom in the practical arts that was necessary for their use of fire. But he did not provide political wisdom, necessary for living together in society, for that was kept by Zeus. Humans were the only animals to command the divine power of fire and its use as a means for their existence. Also, they alone among the animals worshipped the gods.

Because human beings did not possess the art of politics, Zeus feared they might scatter and be destroyed, unable to form cities. He sent Hermes to distribute equally to all humans the virtue of justice, joined with the proper sense of shame. In Plato's account, Zeus thus looks kindly on Prometheus's act. But in another version, given by Cicero in the *Tusculan Disputations* (2.10), Zeus is greatly displeased by Prometheus's theft of this possession of the gods. Cicero quotes from a lost play of Aeschylus in which Zeus (Jove) chains Prometheus to the Caucasus and causes an eagle (Jove's bird) to swoop down and gnaw his liver. His liver grows back daily, only to be continually attacked for centuries, until Jove repeals the punishment.

Whether Zeus acts kindly toward Prometheus's theft for humanity or is furiously offended, the fact remains that human animals, unlike any of the others, possess the divine power of fire, sharing ownership of this element with the gods. Possession of fire allows the human race to do four things, in addition to using it for warmth and protection. First, as claimed by Giambattista Vico, the philosopher of history, humans could set fire to the great forests that cover the earth after the universal flood, in order to accomplish the "heavy task of bringing their lands under cultivation and sowing them with grain, which roasted among the thorns and briers, they had perhaps discovered to be useful for human nourishment."[2] In so doing, these *giganti*, these proto-farmers, accomplish a labor of Hercules and discover the connection of fire to food.

Second, in imitation of Hephaestus (Vulcan), the ancient humans are able to harness the power of nature itself to transform matter from one state to another. As Mircea Eliade, the mythographer and historian of religion puts it: "It is with fire that he controls the passage of matter from one state to another. The first potter who, with the aid of live embers, was successful in hardening those shapes which he had given to his clay, must have felt the intoxication of the demiurge: he had discovered a transmuting agent."[3] Fire puts the cosmic power of nature into human hands.

From the potter comes the smith with the power, by means of forge and crucible, to smelt metals and make tools. Although tool behavior is not exclusive to human animals, the smith is able to make tools that can transform every aspect of human existence, including the cooking and eating of food. From the smith, later, comes the alchemist, who develops elaborate recipes to accomplish "the *opus alchymicum* which haunted the philosophic imagination for more than two thousand years: the idea of the transmutation of man and the Cosmos by means of the Philosopher's

Stone."[4] Through the powers of the potter, smith, and alchemist humans become "masters of fire." In the cook there is always the hint of the alchemist, who knows how to make the whole become more than the parts.

Third, the use of fire in cookery is parallel to its presence in ancient agriculture and fabrication. The most primitive form of cookery is the direct application of fire to food. Vico says: "It is true that Homer describes his heroes as always eating roast meats. This is the simplest and easiest way of cooking them, since it requires nothing but live coals."[5] In the *Republic*, Plato says Homer knew that this way of cooking was the best way to feed soldiers: "for it's easier nearly everywhere to use fire alone than to carry pots and pans" (404c). Vico notes that the banquets of the ancient heroes were always sacrificial in nature. We find this sense of the banquet in the actions of Agamemnon in the *Iliad* (3.264–324). Vico says: "Agamemnon himself, accordingly, kills the two lambs whose sacrifice consecrates the terms of the war with Priam. Such was the magnificence at that time of an idea we would now associate with a butcher!"[6] The practice of pouring a libation to the gods when dining and drinking is preservation of the sense of the sacrifice. Athenaeus says: "It was not unusual, therefore, for ancient cooks to be familiar with sacrificial procedure; at any rate, they were in charge of both wedding feasts and sacrifices" (14.659d).

Fourth, the second major use of fire in cookery is the preparation of food in boiling water. The crucible in which ore is transformed into metal is transferred to the vessel of the cooking pot in which the raw is transformed into the cooked. Vico claims: "Only after this stage [roasting] must have come boiled meats, for in addition to fire they require water, a kettle, and along with it a tripod."[7] In the *Aeneid* Virgil has Aeneas and his men prepare meat by both roasting and boiling (1.208–22). Vico says: "Last of all came seasoned foods, which besides the things already mentioned, called also for condiments."[8]

Condiments include the side-dishes of vegetables that accompany a meat or fish dish, as well as bread, cheese, honey, and fruit. In the *Odyssey*, when Odysseus, returned to Ithaca, sits down with Penelope, he speaks of the prosperity that surrounds them, the result of the leadership of: "some blameless king, who, with the fear of the gods in his heart, is lord over many valiant men, upholding justice; and the black earth bears wheat and barley, and the trees are laden with fruit, the flocks bring forth young unceasingly, and the sea yields fish, all from his good leading; and the people prosper under him" (19.108–14). One is reminded of the frescoes by Ambrogio Lorenzetti, in the Palazzo Pubblico at Siena, contrasting the conditions of life under *buon* and *mal governo* (good and bad government). Under bad government the countryside is bare and barren—the trees have no fruit and no one is cultivating the crops. Prosperity is to live under justice and to have the fields, flocks, and streams full of food, the maintenance of which depends upon a well-ordered society.

The cook is an heir of the divine Promethean gift. By commanding the power of this gift, cooking makes a transition from nature to culture. Humans are the only animals who cook and hence the only animals who eat rather than feed. In creating his city in the *Republic*, the Platonic Socrates says the "first and greatest need is to provide food to sustain life" (369d). The human as the master of fire, in the figure of the cook, generates the institution of the kitchen—or at least the hearth. A kitchen without fire is simply a pantry, a storehouse of foodstuffs. With fire, it is the offspring of the divine precinct.

The Idea of Courses

The acquisition of fire, and the accomplishment of cookery it makes possible, allows humans, like heroes and gods, to engage in banquets. As quoted above, the most comprehensive ancient text on banquets are the fifteen books of the

Deipnosophistai of the Graeco-Egyptian writer Athenaeus of Naucratis (fl. c. A.D. 200).[9] The Deipnosophists, literally, are culinary experts (from *deipnon*, "meal" plus *sophistēs*, "wise men"), those who can apply their wisdom as a source for table talk—"learned banqueters." The banquet described extends over several days, during which a great variety of foodstuffs are consumed and discussed in detail and at length. Mixed with these discussions and descriptions of types of food are discourses on major ideas of humanistic concern.

Those present include four philosophers, four physicians, three musicians (one of whom is specifically a citharode and another is also a poet and jurist), eight grammarians, and a lexicographer. They number more than double the number of Muses. Their views are presented in a symposiac framework, but as integrated with the courses eaten at a banquet. The tradition of the Greek symposium (from *sympinein*, "to drink together") was a drinking party that followed the evening meal, as represented by the masterpiece of Plato's dialogue, the *Symposium*. The work of Athenaeus is the subject of Chapter 3.

Athenaeus's account of the banquet demonstrates the natural interconnection between dining and discourse. We see this connection also in Plutarch's *Septem Sapientium Convivium* (*Dinner of the Seven Wise Men*)—the seven sages of Greece who meet at Delphi to celebrate the dedication of the famous inscriptions on the temple of Apollo—*gnothi seauton* and *mēden agan* ("know thyself" and "nothing overmuch," as well as others that have been lost). At the dinner Cleodorus, answering a question of Solon, says that the dining table is "an altar of the gods of friendship and hospitality" (*Moralia* 158c). This dinner is the subject of Chapter 2.

Dining is distinctive to the human animal, as has been demonstrated. The meal is the purpose of cookery, and the meal requires table manners and conviviality. Dining is a life-ordering experience, with its roots in the ancient sense of the sacrificial—the connection of the human to the gods. The gods conduct banquets and the humans do so in imitation of the gods. One is reminded of "A Fable About Man" by the Spanish Humanist, Juan Luis Vives, that relates a banquet held by Jupiter to celebrate Juno's birthday, at which man, as part of the entertainment, impersonates first plants, then animals, then humans, then the gods, and finally Jupiter himself. The gods are so impressed with this talented playing of these roles, this unique ability of the human being to be an archmime, that they ask man to join them in their seats at the banquet.[10] Dining is in essence a connection to the divine.

Discourse is also distinctive to the human animal. Although non-human animals communicate and manifest some linguistic and proto-linguistic ability, only human animals fully engage in the symbolic act in which meanings build upon themselves to form worlds of ideas and ideals, in which language is even used to have words reflect upon themselves. Language is the key to self-knowledge. We may consider, with Socrates in the *Phaedrus*, whether we are complex creatures, puffed up with pride, like Typhon or are a simpler, gentler being, blessed with a more quiet nature (230a).

Dining is an occasion to exercise the human ability of the word. Humans share the act of nourishment with non-human animals but they do not share with them the art of dining or of putting thought into words. Athenaeus, citing Hesiod, says: "It is nice for people at a meal and a substantial banquet to enjoy conversation, after they have had enough to eat" (2.40f). In the dinner the senses and the intellect are brought together, as they are in the human psyche itself.

The host may follow the ancient precept, often attributed to Marcus Terentius Varro, that at dinner the number of guests should be greater than that of the Graces and less than that of the Muses. A formal dinner-party or a dinner for a special occasion or holiday may be larger. A banquet has no set limits on the number of guests. A dinner has a set number of courses, served in a particular order, but a banquet may expand the number of courses and the number of dishes served in unique and multiple ways. The principle of the banquet is variety and abundance. A dinner is a meal taken on a daily basis; a banquet marks a special occasion. To have a meal in the sense of dining is to eat in a certain way, that is to say, by courses, and, if not eaten alone, is to be accompanied by conversation. Dinner conversation often includes the food itself as subject, for the content of the meal is not to be ignored or simply consumed with indifference.

In his lecture "Delle cene sontuose de' romani" ("On the Sumptuous Dinners of the Romans"), delivered before the Accademia Palatina in Naples in 1699, Vico offers a description of the structure of the Roman meal.[11] He states that he believes the subject of Roman dining can be completely described and explained in terms of four headings: time, place, means, and order of dining. He draws on some of the Latin authors essential to modern accounts of the subject, such as Lucullus, Seneca, Pliny, and Petronius.[12]

As to time, Roman dinners began at the Roman ninth hour (nona, very roughly, three o'clock p.m.), the beginning of the evening. The Romans ate little during the day, taking a full-course, formal meal only in the evening. The place of dining was the cenaculum or upper room of a house. Vico says that the art of dining required not only the means to supply the kitchen—a pantry, a vivarium (to keep animals alive for food), and a piscina (to keep live fish)—but also a librarium (a collection of books). He claims such dinners provided not only food for the body but also food for thought (il corpo coi mangiari, l'animo con le cognizioni). The librarium was nearby to supply books that could be referred to in order to resolve a dispute that might arrive in conversation.

In relation to means, Vico comments on the elaborate nature of the glassware, utensils, and serving pieces employed and on the various images displayed on them that represent types of food. He describes the triclinia, dining couches, arranged on three sides of the low dining table, *mensa*, and on the order of placement of host and guests on each couch. Each couch held three reclining diners. The length of the dining room, *triclinium*, was to be twice its breadth. Vico also describes a second type of dining arrangement—the single, semicircular couch, *stibadium*, that held all the diners around a half-moon shaped *mensa*.

Vico mentions that the diners would have gone to the baths, and from them to dinner, dressed in appropriate togas. In fact, the taking of baths, along with cooking, mark the beginning of civilization. Sacred ablutions precede sacrifices, a custom that Vico holds is common to all nations. The symbolism of water and fire, *aqua* and *igni*, is fundamental to the Roman ceremony of marriage. He mentions that the dinner would include entertainment, especially music and singing. He also mentions the custom of each guest, on leaving, putting tidbits (*apophoreta*) into a napkin, to take home. Works on Roman dining point out that guests would normally bring napkins with them for this purpose, a forerunner of the modern American custom of diners in restaurants requesting to take home uneaten portions of their dinners, in what at one time were called "doggy bags," implying that the remains, especially bones, were to be taken home for the pet dog.

The order of Roman dining was divided into three parts. Vico says the first course (*gustatio*) was called *anticena* or *del mulso*. His reference to *del mulso* is to mead—wine mixed with honey—drunk before the main course for refreshment, a recipe for which is the first entry in the book of Apicius (see chapter 4). The first course or appetizer has precedent in Greek dining, as evident in the elaborate discussion of it by Athenaeus in Book 2 of his work (58b ff.). The drinking of flavored wine corresponds to the modern aperitif. The *anticena* could be an assortment of small portions of vegetables, fish and shellfish, and cuts of meat and fowl, including the famous roasted dormice in honey sauce, and perhaps employing the distinctively Roman preparation of *garum*, the fish paste similar to modern anchovy sauce, the use of which can be found in the book of Apicius. The translator of *Apicius de re coquinaria* states: "A real platter of *hors d'oevres*, an *antipasto* is not complete unless made according to certain Apician precepts."[13]

The main course or *mensa* proper, as Vico points out, could contain all the luxurious sorts of foods made in elaborate presentation for which the Romans became famous. Vico mentions dishes of exotic fish, brains of pheasants, parrot tongues, and so forth. Although he is clear about the decadence of the exotic dishes served at Roman dinners, Vico also sees there is something grand and civilized about the idea of these dinners.

The third part of the dinner, *secundae mensae*, was dessert, consisting of an assortment of fruits, and sweets made with honey, for, as Vico rightly points out, the Romans did not use sugar. According to modern authorities the dessert course might also include something similar to what in British cookery is called a "savory." Vico says that the laws of drinking were, to drink wine at first in the amount of what would today be a glass, but toward the dinner's end to change to drink amounts equal to three of our glasses. Toasts would be made to themselves, to friends, to the gods, and to Augustus. The first drink would be dedicated to Jove, and to Mercury a drink would be dedicated with the first dish of meat. In departing, as mentioned above, guests would fill their napkins with what they wished to take home, and would wish each other *Buon pro* ("Good health") and extend to the host good luck from heaven.

A topic to which Vico makes reference but does not discuss in detail is the custom of the *larva convivialis*, the articulated skeleton, often made of wood or ivory that the host might call for in the middle of dinner. Vico notes that in the *Cena Trimalchionis* of Petronius a skeleton made of silver is brought out. This custom, apparently of Egyptian origin, was designed to remind the diners that the joys of the body are brief. In describing Egyptian dining customs, Herodotus says: "At rich men's banquets, after dinner a man carries round a wooden image of a corpse in a coffin, painted and carved in exact imitation, a cubit or two cubits long. This he shows to each of the company, saying, 'Drink and make merry, but look on this; for such shalt thou be when thou art dead.' Such is the custom at their drinking-bouts" (278). Goblets and mosaics in the Roman *triclinium* were decorated with skulls and skeletons.

Home Cooking

I take the title of this work from Pellegrino Artusi's classic, *La scienza in cucina e l'arte di mangiar bene*. Its frontispiece announces that his book combines hygiene, economy, and good taste in a practical manual for the family.[14] In it are 790 recipes, with instructions, often accompanied by little narratives. The recipes are followed by menus for each month of the year, including suggestions for special holiday and feast meals. Artusi's concern is to show that *buon gusto* and *buona salute*, good taste and good health, can be combined. It is a nineteenth-century work, written in the Tuscan tradition of "*La buona, sana cucina.*" Artusi (1820–1910), born in Forlimpopolo, near Bologna, moved to Tuscany in 1851, undertook the work as a project of his retirement. He published it at his own expense in 1891, because his friends advised him that such a book had no future. He dedicated it to his two white cats—Biancani and Sibillone. It became a bestseller, appearing in fourteen editions during his lifetime.

Artusi intersperses his recipes with little stories and comments. For example, he introduces his recipe for *salsa di pomodoro* (tomato sauce) with this little narrative. "There was a priest in Romagna who put his nose into everything; introducing himself into families, he wished to have his finger in every domestic affair. He was, however, an honest man and because of his conscientiousness he generated more good than bad in whatever he was allowed to do; the populace argued to name him *Don Pomodoro* to indicate that tomatoes can enter into everything, because a good sauce of this fruit will be a valuable aid in the kitchen."[15] Chapter 4 will discuss at greater length both Artusi's book and that of Apicius.

Giuliano Bugialli, in his extraordinary cookbook of Florentine dining, says: "While Apicius' book gives us the elaborate dishes of the upper class of the Empire, there was a simpler cooking, which ordinary people ate every day, and this, like many aspects of Roman culture, came from the Etruscans, the people who inhabited Tuscany and whose descendants still live there."[16] Indeed, in the depictions on Etruscan sarcophagi we see a people dining and enjoying themselves. Athenaeus writes: "In Etruria, sumptuous tables are set twice a day, along with couches spread with brightly colored cloths and silver drinking vessels of every type" (4.153d).

Bugialli explains that the courses of the meal eaten today in Florence are consistent with those of the sixteenth century: "In the sixteenth century the Florentines started their search for the lightest possible, the most healthy, the most elegantly simple cooking—a search that has continued to the present day."[17] Michelangelo or Galileo could enter a traditional Tuscan *trattoria* today and, without looking at a menu, request what they wished to eat, and it would without hesitation be served to them.

Bugialli further points out that in sixteenth-century Florence, "for the first time in the modern West, there was a fixed order of courses and many defined conventions for formal dining."[18] The meal began, then as today, with *antipasti*, a series of appetizers (*antipasto* means before the *pasto*, or meal). The first full course of the meal was the boiled course, which could be one or more of a variety of boiled dishes. This course, by the beginning of the nineteenth century, had become the *minestra* or soup course, and by the end of the century pasta had made its way north from southern Italy. The two forms of eating pasta—*pasta in brodo* (in broth) and *pasta asciutta* (pasta with sauce) preserve the boiled course. Bugialli notes that the three-pronged fork was invented to make it possible to eat spaghetti without using the hands. It is by now commonly known that Marco Polo did not introduce pasta to Italy. Noodles are made and used in various dishes in many culinary traditions, but pasta is a unique Italian possession.[19]

In the introduction to their excellent work on the *Medieval Kitchen*, the authors state, regarding the use of forks and napkins, that: "From the fourteenth century on, the Priors (as members of the government were called) of Florence had their own individual napkins and cutlery, including a fork. This was a level of luxury that did not spread to the rest of Europe for another two or three hundred years. We recall that Henri III (1551–89) and his favorites were savagely taunted for preferring to eat with forks, and, at the very dawn of the Enlightenment, Louis XIV always displayed regal scorn for that intermediary between him and his food, which diminished his dining pleasure."[20] In medieval dining in northern Europe, even strangers often ate by sharing a trencher or *tailloir*, with a spoon used to dip sauce from a shared bowl, taking morsels of food by hand, picking them up with three fingers to lift to the mouth. Good manners dictated not to overeat, grab food, or choose the best pieces.

The second course, Bugialli says, was of fried or roasted dishes, followed by the third course of fruit, which in the sixteenth century could also include vegetables. For instance, even today fennel may be eaten raw at the end of a meal. Today vegetable dishes accompany the second course as *contorni* (literally "contours") or side dishes, served on a small plate, separate from that for the meat, fish, or poultry. The *antipasto* and three courses constitute a complete meal, a tetralogy.

The home-cooked meal of the Florentine-Tuscan kitchen today can require no more than an hour, an hour well spent, given the enjoyment and nutrition it produces. This preparation time can presuppose a sauce or meat from a roast or another ingredient done at another time, but the use of leisure for the preparation and availability of that item is well worth it. For an everyday Florentine meal one might prepare an antipasto of a simple salad of *carote all'agro* (raw, shredded carrots in lemon juice and olive oil), or slices of *fettunta* (toasted bread rubbed with fresh garlic and dressed with warm olive oil), or *fagioli, tonno e cipolle* (cannellini beans combined with tuna, red onions, and olive oil), or a *frittata al basilico* (frittata with basil).

For *il primo* one might consider a pasta with *briciolata* (a sauce of bread crumbs lightly browned in olive oil with salt and pepper, but without grated cheese), or with *pommorola* (a summer sauce of cooked tomatoes and vegetables, parsley, and basil, passed through a food mill and served with grated *parmigiano-reggiano*), or *taglierini al limone* (a sauce of butter, cream, lemon peel, nutmeg, and *parmigiano*, served over fresh pasta, with parsley), or *penne alle olive nere* (a sauce of *prosciutto*, *porcini* mushrooms, black olives, tomatoes, served over *penne lisce*—the form of *penne* pasta of special preference in Florence).

For *il secondo*, perhaps a slice of previously prepared *Arista* (roast pork loin with garlic, rosemary, and black pepper), accompanied by *rape saltate in padella* (a cooked green, sautéed in garlic and oil), or *spinaci saltati* (cooked spinach sautéed in garlic and oil), or perhaps *pesce al cartoccio* (a whole fish baked in parchment paper or aluminum foil, with rosemary and garlic), accompanied by *fagiolini in fricassea* (small stringbeans, in lemon-egg sauce), or *petti di pollo alla Fiorentina* (chicken breasts sautéed with artichokes), or *polpette di bistecca in umido* (coarsely chopped beef "sausages," sautéed, served in tomato sauce, accompanied by *finocchi al burro* (fennel sautéed in butter).

That course usually would be followed by assorted fresh fruit of the season. If strawberries or peaches were available they might be mixed with sugar and lemon and immersed in Chianti wine. Pears might be poached in red wine and tawny port. For a Sunday or more special meal, a pastry-based or other sweet dessert might be made, such as *crostata di frutta* (assorted fresh fruit with a cream *pasticcera* in a pastry shell). A salad might be included in the meal, and would be dressed first by lightly salting the leaves, then coating them with olive oil, and finally adding a small amount of vinegar. There is no "main" course in an Italian meal.

There can be a cheese course, but not necessarily. At a very formal dinner, it replaces the fruit course. A *risotto* might be the *primo* course instead of pasta. Risotto or pasta is not eaten as a side dish or combined with the *secondo*, as so often found in American restaurants today. What I have described as the Florentine meal can have many variations, all within a set pattern that allows for a certain amount of *fantasia*, but the mixing together of the *primo* and *secondo* of a meal is invalid.

In an elaborate or formal Florentine dinner there can also be a *piatto di mezzo*, or in-between course, coming between the first full course (*primo piatto*) and the second course (*secondo piatto*). This *piatto di mezzo* can be a *sformato*, a vegetable dish involving *balsamella*. Before dinner there can be *aperitivi*, and after dinner, *digestivi* (liqueurs) as well as coffee. To comprehend the principles of the cuisine of one of the Italian cities is to have access to the cuisine of all the cities, as their differences are variations on one another. And to comprehend Italian cuisine is to grasp the basic concepts of food and wine that extend throughout the Mediterranean.

We live in an age in which a meal of several simple courses is not a matter of daily life. Family eating has become family feeding. Something is eaten, in some way or another, and is called dinner. To dine requires retreat to a full-service restaurant, run by a chef. To eat under these conditions requires participation in a kind of high nonsense—of relating to wait-staff, considering "chef's specials," examining minute descriptions of plates that can be ordered, taking in various "food concepts" and themes in which the restaurant envelops itself—all the décor, paraphernalia, and pseudo-content of "dining out." Instead of each dish being served on its own plate, as in Florentine cuisine, the diner is most likely faced with "stacked" food. Anything to be ordered from the menu is a creation of the chef, with five, six, or more things piled together on a plate—a portion of fish or meat placed over a portion of a "starch" with a sauce beneath it, topped with a vegetable, perhaps prepared in another sauce, and surmounting this may be a sprig of an herb or two, with a streak of another sauce on the open space of the plate—and so forth.

All of this is someone's idea of eating. There is no national tradition of eating or cooking that justifies stacked food. Culinary traditions involve combinations of foods but they do not support the hodgepodge of items created by contemporary chefs *ex nihilo*. An example of bad dining is the recent mania of involving goat cheese in every way possible, as if its presence guaranteed sophistication. I much agree with Bugialli's comment, that although goat cheese has existed in Italy for centuries, there is not a single dish that uses it cooked. As he says: "This is not because no one has ever thought of cooking it, but because the change in taste and strong smell of the heated cheese has been consciously rejected. It is my opinion that cooked goat cheese is a culinary travesty."[21] To eat in a restaurant these days, except for one that offers simple, direct fare, is to prove the truth of the French saying: *"On ne mange bien que chez soi"*—"One eats best, who eats at home."

Stacked food, processed food, and fast food form a continuum. They are engineered food, a product of the technological mindset that strives unceasingly for novelty, for the new. Their newly formed combinations of ingredients are analogous to gimmicks, as distinguished from real inventions. Gimmicks are the result of a fascination with performance. They respond to no real need or idea. Traditional cuisine, that alters itself only over time, rests on the repetition of dishes. A true dish, like a poem, musical composition, or work of art, can be enjoyed over and over. It has the power of repetition. Most recipes of the Italian table rarely require more than five simple ingredients. The dishes they produce are eaten for generations without anyone tiring of them.

A final word can be said, about the eating of spaghetti. To observe a patron of a restaurant attacking a bowl of spaghetti, employing a large spoon in tandem with a fork as a means of taking the spaghetti from the bowl to the mouth, is to witness a modern *commedia dell' arte*. Eating spaghetti in this manner is unknown in Italy. How did this strange form of eating come about? One theory is that, when spaghetti first appeared in America, it was served on plates. Since plates have no rim, as do shallow bowls, against which contour to twirl the strands with the fork, a spoon was used as a substitute. I do not find this explanation plausible. Shallow soup bowls have been available for generations, and spaghetti as well as soup is served in them. The only explanation of which I can think is analogous to the reply given by Samuel Johnson, author of the great *Dictionary*, when asked by a lady why he defined "pastern" as the "knee" of a horse. Dr. Johnson replied: "Ignorance, madam, pure ignorance."[22] In the case of the large-spoon eating of spaghetti, it is ignorance posing as sophistication.

The Physiology of Taste

The science of cookery is connected to that of chemistry and the art of eating well is connected to that of medicine.

Joseph Dommers Vehling, the translator of Apicius, says: "It is well-known that in chemistry (cookery is but applied chemistry) the knowledge of the rules governing the quantities and the sequence of ingredients, their manipulation, either separately or jointly, either successively or simultaneously, is a very important matter, and that violation or ignorance of the process any spell failure at any stage of the experiment. In the kitchen this is particularly true of baking and soup and sauce making, the most intricate of culinary operations."[23] Cookery and chemistry in its classic form certainly share in the need to know the nature of substances and the principles by which they can be combined. The advantage of cookery over chemistry is that its results, when properly produced, offer a delight of the senses, whereas chemistry, as Schopenhauer said, can affect the senses as just "bad cooking." The delight that results from chemical experiment is the knowledge of nature, not the odors involved.

Cooking, because of its relation to nutrition, is a constant companion to medicine as the care of the body. Artusi added an appendix on "La cucina per gli stomachi deboli" (Cooking for Weak Stomachs), describing those foods and their preparation that are acceptable for those who have delicate digestion. A diet adjusted to the state of one's health is the basis for preventing disease and maintenance of the body. These concerns are shared by the art of good eating and medicine as it strives to prevent disease. The art of eating well must be concerned above all with digestion, as expressed in the Florentine view that "good food is never filling" (does not overload the digestion).

In the *Timaeus* we find a comparison of digestion with respiration: "The fire cuts up the food [in our bellies] and as it follows the breath it oscillates inside us. As the oscillation goes on, the fire pumps the cut-up bits of food from the belly and packs them into the veins. This is the mechanism by which the streams of nourishment continue to flow throughout the bodies of all living things" (80d).

Galen could well agree, as he says in *On the Natural Faculties*: "It is quite clear, therefore, that nutrition must necessarily be a process of assimilation of that which is nourishing to that which is being nourished. Some, however, say that this assimilation does not occur in reality, but is merely apparent; these are the people who think that Nature is not artistic, that she does not show forethought for the animal's welfare, and that she has absolutely no native powers whereby she alters some substances, attracts others, and discharges others" (1.12.26–27). Greek medicine is based on moderation; health, like art, requires proportion. The courses of the Greco-Roman meal keep all foods in proportion, both in what is eaten and how it is eaten.

Jean-Anthelme Brillat-Savarin, in the *Physiologie du goût* (*The Physiology of Taste*) (1825) brings together the aesthetic, chemical, and medical senses of gastronomy of his time. It is a wide-ranging work, treating almost every aspect of things of the table, infused with Brillat-Savarin's fascination with the new science of chemistry. The work begins with a list of twenty aphorisms, announced as providing "an eternal foundation of his Science."[24] The first of these aphorisms is: "The world is nothing without life, and all that lives takes nourishment." The fourth is: "Tell me what you eat: I will tell you what you are." The ninth is: "The discovery of a new dish does more for the happiness of mankind than the discovery of a star." The eleventh is: "The right order of eating is from the most substantial dishes to the lightest." The sixteenth is: "The most indispensable quality of a cook is punctuality; it is also that of a guest." And the twentieth is: "To entertain a guest is to make yourself responsible for his happiness so long as he is beneath your roof."

Regarding digestion, Brillat-Savarin says: "'Man lives not on what he eats, but on what he digests,' says an old proverb. We must therefore digest to live."[25] He proceeds to give a detailed description of the process, including how digestion affects the mental state of the individual. He understands the interconnection of the use of language and dining: "It was the meal which was responsible for the birth, or at least the elaboration of languages, not only because it was a continually recurring occasion for meetings, but also because the leisure which accompanies and succeeds the meal is naturally conducive to confidence and loquacity."[26] He advocates gourmandism as an ideal, holding that "social gourmandism combines the elegance of Athens, the luxury of Rome, and the delicacy of France. . . . a precious quality, which might well be called a virtue, and is at least the source of our purest pleasures."[27] Gourmandism is one of the highest human pursuits, and at least is the necessary complement to all other distinctive and great human endeavors.

Taste is the essence of gourmandism. It is the sense that brings together the other four. Taste is defined as "that one of our senses which puts us in contact with palatable bodies by means of the sensation which they arouse in the organ designed to judge them."[28] Gourmandism is above all the agency of taste: "Gourmandism is an impassioned, reasoned, and habitual preference for everything which gratifies the organ of taste."[29] Brillat-Savarin, however, is clear that gourmandism is the enemy of excess. It is not the pursuit of eating simply to consume whatever can be had or to drink to excess. The pleasure of the table is to eat well and this requires a knowledge of food, a grasp of how it should be prepared and served, and a sense above all of the aesthetic. Eating well is an art upon which the good life depends.

Brillat-Savarin (although not referring to the view expressed by Athenaeus, citing Hesiod, quoted above) agrees that conversation begins once initial appetite has been satisfied at a meal. He says: "At the beginning of the meal, and throughout the first course, each guest eats steadily, without speaking or paying attention to anything which may be said. . . . But when the need for food begins to be satisfied, then the intellect awakes, talk becomes general, a new order of things is initiated, and he who until then was a mere consumer of food, becomes a table companion of more or less charm, according to the qualities bestowed on him by the Master of all things."[30]

The natural order of dining is to allow the appetite, guided by the senses, to dominate and then, as their domination subsides, conversation, the medium of sociability, takes shape. The purpose of dining is not simply to eat. Conversation, if it is to be more than shallow exchange, requires some learning and mental acumen. It above all requires imagination, which, as Aristotle holds, is memory. Since there is nothing in memory that is not first in the senses, memory is the source of what is brought forth in the imagination. Learning depends on memory and when what is learned is brought forth, ingenuity, what in Latin is *ingenium*, is required to form it in a manner that makes for conversation. A dinner is interesting and rewarding to the spirit if the food is good and the guests are thoughtful.

In his discussion of the "pleasures of the table," Brillat-Savarin delineates the conditions necessary for a proper dinner party. He advances the question of how to procure the pleasures of the table in the highest degree. He says: "That question I am about to answer. Compose yourselves, readers, and pay attention; Gasterea inspires me, the prettiest of all the Muses; I shall be clearer than an oracle, and my precepts will go down the ages."[31] He provides the reader with twelve such precepts. "Gasterea" (from Greek *gastero* – belly) is Brillat-Savarin's own Muse, not one of Hesiod's list.

The first of these precepts is that the guests should not be more than twelve, to facilitate conversation. They should be of different occupations, but with similar tastes. The dining-room should be "well-lighted, the cloth impeccably white, and the atmosphere maintained at a temperature of from sixty to seventy degrees." The men should be witty and the women charming (in stating this, he notes that he is "writing this in Paris, between the Palais-Royal and the Chaussée-d'Antin"). The dishes should be few in number but choice and well chosen, with wines of the first quality. By this precept he makes clear that the purpose of the meal is to eat certain things in a certain order, not simply to eat all sorts of things. The service of the dishes should proceed from the most substantial to the lightest, and the accompanying wines from the mildest to the most complex. I do not think Brillat-Savarin intends the appetizer or first course to be more substantial than the courses that follow. Instead, I think, the principle is that once the main course is attained, it should not be followed by more substantial courses. In a French meal, once the crescendo has been reached, the dinner should proceed prudently.

The progress of the meal, he says, should be slow so as to "let the guests conduct themselves like travellers due to reach their destination together." Then coffee should be served, piping hot, and the liqueurs well chosen. The diners then retire to the drawing-room, where those "who cannot do without it" can play cards and others may engage in post-prandial conversations. The guests should be encouraged to linger, "sustained by the hope that the evening will not pass without some further pleasure."

Coffee, on Brillat-Savarin's concept, is the end of the dinner but not the end of the evening. The further pleasure is the serving of tea, toast, and punch: "Let the tea be not too strong, the toast artistically buttered, and the punch mixed with proper care." This coda is, to my knowledge, unique; unknown in Mediterranean or modern dining generally, but perhaps customary to Parisian dining of Brillat-Savarin's day. Judging from his remarks, he seems personally very fond of the buttered toast and punch service. His final precept is to "Let retirement begin not earlier than eleven o'clock, but by midnight let everyone be in bed."

The pleasures of the table can thus be of lengthy duration. The important principle is that everyone eats well but does not overeat, so that everyone retires peacefully into bed, to arise the next morning without hangover or discomfort. Of his twelve precepts, Brillat-Savarin concludes: "Whoever has been present at a meal fulfilling all these conditions may claim to have witnessed his own apotheosis; and for each of them which is forgotten or ignored, the guests will suffer a proportionate decrease of pleasure."[32] These precepts, then, state the ethic of gourmandism.

Brillat-Savarin's gourmandism has a resonance with Epicureanism, as likely do the views of all who endorse the pleasures of the table. Epicurus distinguished between "kinetic" pleasures such as eating choice foods, and "catastematic" pleasures such as not being hungry. Kinetic pleasures come and go; they must continually be renewed. Catastematic pleasures are achieved by the prolonged good state of the body, the enjoyment of good health.

The pleasures of the mind can also be kinetic, in the sense of recording pleasant rather than painful sensations. The catastematic pleasure of the mind is achieved with the prolonged removal of pain and cares that disturb the sense of well-being. The catastematic pleasure of the mind is *ataraxia* or peace of mind, freedom from passion, calmness. In Epicurean doctrine, *ataraxia* is achieved when the study of natural philosophy relieves one of the fear of the gods and when death is recognized as natural. But it is also sustained by storing up memories of past pleasures, of past conversations, and of friendships. Applied to Brillat-Savarin's ideal of gourmandism, the pleasures of the table can greatly contribute to the catastematic pleasure of *ataraxia*, as well as the kinetic pleasures of the senses. The art of eating well not only pleases the palate, it promotes friendships with those who share the table, and, when done properly, promotes the well-being and memories that support peace of mind.

Although Brillat-Savarin defines taste in physiological terms, behind his view, and especially involved in his ethic of gourmandism, is the broader sense of taste as it resides in aesthetics. Taste in this sense is motivated by a pursuit of judgment or discernment that arises from an intuitive sense or *je ne sais quoi* of rightness of judgment.

To have taste in food, to have taste in art, and to have taste in all matters of life is the basis of knowing how to live. It requires a kind of prudence joined with pleasure. This sense of taste as a guide to life is easily lost in a world dominated by the matter at hand, the work to be done, progress to be made. The acquisition of taste, like the acquisition of knowledge, requires leisure. It also requires sociability, for taste as a rightness of judgment is not properly a solitary matter; it is formed and expressed in exchange with others. It is style, and style is always the product of order, of a certain way of doing things.

Taste can be learned only in the company of others, and one of the prime forms of this company is the human act of dining. Taste is refined in solitude, as is learning, but it is brought forth in commonality with others who understand the role and need for taste in the conduct of life. If the school of literature is that of the poets, the school of taste as a guide to life is that of the conviviality of the table, at which so much of what is human comes together.

Chapter 2

The Dinner of the Seven Wise Men

Who shall possess the tripod? Thus
replies Apollo: "Whosoever is most
wise." Accordingly they gave it to
Thales, and he to another, and so on
till it comes to Solon, who with the
remark that the god was most wise,
sent it off to Delphi.

Diogenes Laertius *1.28.*

The Dinner

The essay of Plutarch (ca. AD 45–120), *Septem Sapientium Convivium* (*Dinner of the Seven Wise Men*) has already been cited in Chapter 1. It is one of the large collection of Plutarch's writings known as *Moralia* or Moral Essays.[1] *Moralis* is a word formed by Cicero from *mos*, in the sense of custom or regular practice. From it is derived the English word "mores," the morally binding customs of a particular group, the embodiments of their moral attitudes defining their sense of *decorum* or propriety. The seven wise men of ancient Greece are thought to be the authors, or at least the advocates, of the precepts inscribed on the *pronaos* of the Temple of Apollo at Delphi, greeting the visitor and offering instructions for life.

If we ask what is wisdom—that which the seven sages possess—we may also turn to Cicero, as he defines it in the *Tusculan Disputations*: "Wisdom [*sapientia*] is the knowledge of things divine and human and acquaintance with the cause of each of them" (4.26.57). In his work on ethics, *De officiis*,

Cicero repeats this claim and adds that this is the way *sapientia* has been defined "by the philosophers of old" (2.2.5). This definition of wisdom endorsed by the philosophers of old was also to be found in Varro's now lost work on *The Antiquities of Divine and Human Institutions*. In the *Apology*, Socrates presumes this definition when he declares that he possesses human wisdom but not divine wisdom (20 d–e). Although denying he has divine wisdom, Socrates proceeds to justify his activity by asserting that God has assigned him to the city to be its gadfly (30e). Socrates thus has at least enough knowledge of the divine order of things to comprehend this assignment.

Plutarch's essay is an imaginative account of the gathering of the seven sages at Delphi that goes back to Plato's description of it in the *Protagoras* (343a–e). There was a tradition that the gathering was originally to dedicate the inscriptions on the temple and that later there was a dinner hosted by Periander, ruler of Corinth (627–585 BC). On some lists of the seven sages Periander appears as the seventh, but in Plutarch's account he functions as the host of the dinner at Corinth. In Plutarch's account of the dinner he adds other characters to the traditional seven, such as Aesop and two women, Melissa (wife of Periander) and Eumetis or Cleobulina (daughter of Cleobulus of Lindus in Rhodes, one of the seven wise men). There is also Neiloxenus of Naucratis in Egypt, an intimate of Solon and Thales, who escorts them and the others to the dinner.

Plutarch names, as the seven wise men: Thales of Miletus in Asia Minor (c. 636–546), Bias of Priene in Asia Minor (c. 550), Pittacus of Mytilene in Lesbos (c. 650–570), Solon, the Athenian lawgiver (638?–?559), Chilon of Lacedaemon (c. 500), Cleobulus of Lindus in Rhodes (early 6th century), and Anacharsis, a Scythian (c. 594), visiting Athens at the time of Solon. (Plato's list in the *Protagoras* puts Myson of Chen in place of Anacharsis.) Plato makes much of the claim that these seven were admirers of Spartan culture, especially of laconic speech (*lakōnikos*), of which the

Delphic inscriptions of *gnothi seauton* (know thyself) and *mēden agan* (nothing overmuch) are leading examples.

Plutarch's essay is framed as an account given to someone named Nicarchus by a narrator, who identifies himself as being "on intimate terms with Periander by virtue of my profession" (which was likely a seer, versed in ritual purification) (146c) and as the host of Thales, "for he stayed at my house by command of Periander" (146c). Subsequently the narrator is addressed as Diocles (e.g., 149d, 151f, 155d, and 162c). Nicarchus appears to be a younger companion, as the narrator says his reason for relating an account of the gathering is that age is upon him and "that the lapse of time will bring about much obscurity and complete uncertainty regarding actual events, if at the present time, in the case of events so fresh and recent, false accounts that have been concocted obtain credence" (146b). The narrator claims to have been present at the dinner and that he will relate it without any omissions. Plutarch's imaginative account now takes on the form of a true story about events of which we, its readers, have only heard.

The narrator says that in the first place "the dinner was not a dinner of the Seven alone, as you and your friends have been told, but of more than twice that number, including myself" (146c). More than fourteen, for this evening, is not a proper number of guests for a dinner. Even Brillat-Savarin's principles do not allow for more than twelve, as cited in Chapter 1 herein, and it is far greater than that of more than the Graces but less than the Muses. The term in the title of Plutarch's essay, in Greek, is *symposion*, and in Latin *convivium*. The gathering might be best thought of as an elegant dinner party or a small banquet, much smaller than the twenty-four persons at the banquet of Athenaeus or at any festival banquet. It was, however, not held in the royal house of Periander but in a dining-hall near the shrine of Aphrodite.

Neiloxenus, in escorting the group to dinner, precipitates an argumentative conversation concerning the difference between kings and despots and their manner of ruling, which causes Thales to conclude that the discussion should cease, as it is "a conversation that is quite inappropriate, since he [Neiloxenus] has not been careful to bring up topics and questions suitable for persons on their way to dinner" (147e). One is reminded of the prohibition, when dining at high table at Oxford, against talk of politics, religion, or one's own work.

Having chided their escort, Thales asks: "Do you not honestly believe that, as some preparation is necessary on the part of the man who is to be host, there should also be some preparation of the part of him who is to be a guest at dinner?" (147e). Thales says he understands that people in Sybaris present invitations to women for dinner a year in advance so as to allow them opportunity to determine what clothes and jewelry they wish to wear (cf. Athenaeus, 521c). He says he is of the opinion that, on the part of the man, to be the right kind of guest for dinner requires even a longer time, inasmuch as it requires more time for the proper adornment of character than for that of the body. He says: "In fact, the man of sense who comes to dinner does not betake himself there just to fill himself up as though he were a sort of pot, but to take some part, be it serious or humorous, and to listen and to talk regarding this or that topic as the occasion suggests it to the company, if their association together is to be pleasant" (147f).

Thales says that, at dinner, an unsavory dish or a poor wine can be passed over, but an unpleasant guest can cause unpleasantness and animosity to last a lifetime. He says Chilon demonstrated excellent judgment by not agreeing to come to the dinner until he had learned the name of everyone invited. By knowing with whom one is to dine, one can be prepared to engage in mutual interests and not simply be placed in the position one is in when having to trust to luck as to the persons one finds oneself with on shipboard or serving in the army.

In regard for the importance of the need for mutual friendliness at table, Thales mentions the Egyptian custom of showing the skeleton or *larva convivialis* to the guests at dinner (see the comment on this custom in Chapter 1, herein). Thales may mention this especially because Neiloxenus is from Naucratis in Egypt. He says that although the appearance of this omen of mortality may be unsettling, it is appropriate for the diners to see "if it urges upon them that life, which is short in point of time, should not be made long by evil conduct" (148b). Plutarch, through the speech of Thales, takes very seriously the importance of table-talk for friendship. At table, time seems suspended, but the appearance of the *larva convivialis* reminds us that it is not stopped.

As they arrive at the dining hall, an issue is raised concerning where one is seated by the host. Thales counsels that when seated in one's assigned place we should not ask who is seated at a higher or lower place than ourselves, but we should try to discover in those seated with us "something that may serve to initiate and keep up friendship" (149a–b). To prove his point, Thales, on entering the dining hall, takes an inferior place, to which one of the lesser guests had raised objection. The discussion of seating raises the issue that at a dinner party, even today, there should be a seating plan, perhaps with place cards, decided upon by the host. To tell one's guests to sit just anywhere is improper, and thus discourteous. It is equally so to complain as to where one is seated by one's host. The type of friendship one has with one's assigned dinner companions is what Aristotle designates as friendship of utility. This is a friendship that originates between persons having a condition in common. Another example of a friendship of utility is the temporary friendship between persons finding themselves traveling together.

What is served at the dinner is not described. The narrator reports that "the dinner was plainer than usual." Although Periander was known to be capable of elaborate and expensive dinners and entertainment, "on this occasion he tried to make an impression on the men by simplicity and restraint in expenditure" (150c–d). He also had his wife appear in modest attire rather than her usual elaborate dress. The tables are cleared and the entertainment is limited to a flute-girl playing a brief accompaniment while the libations are poured. The purpose of the dinner was not the food or wine served, or the entertainment, but the intellectual discussion that was to follow. The body is to be nourished well but the higher purpose of the dinner is the nourishment of the mind. To bring the very founders of Greek culture together requires a celebration of their ideas, a display of their wisdom.

On Government

The discussion is begun by Neiloxenus, reading aloud a letter by Amasis, king of the Egyptians, addressed to Bias, calling him the wisest of the Greeks. The letter begins: "The king of the Ethiopians is engaged in a contest of wisdom against me. Repeatedly vanquished in all else, he has crowned his efforts by framing an extraordinary and awful demand, bidding me to drink up the ocean" (151b). Should Amasis succeed he will be given rule over many villages and cities of the Ethiopians. If not, Amasis is to cede towns now under his control. If Bias can provide a solution, he and his friends will receive whatever is right for them from the Egyptian king.

Bias offers the solution, which is for Amasis to "tell the Ethiopian to stop the rivers which are now emptying into the ocean depths, while he himself is engaged in drinking up the ocean that now is; for this is the ocean with which the demand is concerned, and not the one which is to be" (151d). Apparently this solution presupposes that the water in the ocean is naturally being drained off but at the same time replenished by the rivers that flow into it. So, should the king of the Ethiopians comply he would have unwittingly solved his own problem.

Bias has given the answer to the question, but Periander adds that they should all contribute an offering to the king.

In so saying Periander is thinking of the scene in the *Odyssey* in which Alcinous, king of the Phaeacians, proposes that each of those who frequents his palace give Odysseus a gift before he sails on his final journey to his own Ithaca. Alcinous says: "But come now, let us give him a great tripod and a cauldron, each man of us" (13.10–15). The seven wise men do not produce material gifts, but, in accord with their nature, they produce their gifts of wisdom. Solon the lawgiver says that a king would best gain repute "if out of a monarchy he should organize a democracy for his people" (152a). Bias adds that the king should be the very first to conform to his country's laws.

Thales says that happiness (*eudaimonia*) for a ruler is to reach old age and die a natural death. This advice points to the fact that most rulers or despots die by the sword, the means by which they became kings. It resonates also with the view, expressed later by Aristotle in his *Ethics*, that no person can be said to be happy until the person's life is over. And it is best to have a complete life. Anacharsis adds that dying a natural death requires the ruler to have sound sense, that is, not to take undue use of his power. Cleobulus says that if a ruler wishes to live to a natural death he must trust none of his associates. Pittacus says a full life is possible, "If the ruler should manage to make his subjects fear, not him, but for him" (152b). Chilon says that a ruler's thoughts should be not those of a mortal but of an immortal. The ruler, then, should be seen by his subjects as capable of what is otherwise found only in the gods. Periander, himself a ruler, is asked to add his view to that of the Seven. He says: "Well, I may add my view, that the opinions expressed, taken as a whole, practically divorce any man possessed of sense from being a ruler" (152b). Aesop adds that Thales' view would bid a ruler to grow old as fast as possible.

Neiloxenus is then asked to reveal the rest of the letter of Amasis, in which the Ethiopian king gave answers to a series of questions that had been put to him. These were the questions and the Ethiopian's answers:

(a) 'What is the oldest thing?' 'Time.'
(b) 'What is the greatest?' 'The universe.'
(c) 'What is the wisest?' 'Truth.'
(d) 'What is the most beautiful?' 'Light.'
(e) 'What is most common?' 'Death.'
(f) 'What is most helpful?' 'God.'
(g) 'What is most harmful?' 'An evil spirit.'
(h) 'What is strongest?' 'Fortune.'
(i) 'What is easiest?' 'Pleasure' (153a).

Thales offers a critique of each of these answers, saying that they all contain errors and are evidences of ignorance. For example, Thales points out, time cannot be the oldest thing, for if time is divided into past, present, and future, what is in the future would be younger than what is in the present. Regarding death, Thales says that death is not most common because it is not common to the living, thinking of the principle of Epicurus, that death is nothing to those who are alive. Thales then repeats the list, with his answers, with which the others express agreement.

(a) 'What is the oldest thing?' 'God, for God is something that has no beginning.'
(b) 'What is greatest?' 'Space; for while the universe contains within it all else, this contains the universe.'
(c) 'What is most beautiful?' 'The Universe; for everything that is ordered as it should be is a part of it.'
(d) 'What is wisest?' 'Time; for it has discovered some things already, and shall discover all the rest.'
(e) 'What is most common?' 'Hope; for those who have nothing else have that ever with them.'
(f) 'What is most helpful?' 'Virtue; for it makes everything else helpful by putting it to a good use.'
(g) 'What is most harmful?' 'Vice; for it harms the greatest number of things by its presence.'
(h) 'What is strongest?' 'Necessity; for that alone is insuperable.'

(i) 'What is easiest?' 'To follow Nature's course; because people often weary of pleasures.'

The barbarian king has no wisdom. His answers are those that would come to someone who knows only how to think politically and who wishes to act as if wise. Thales reassigns several of the Ethiopian's answers to other questions, that is, God, the Universe, and Time. He answers the questions regarding what is strongest with the exact opposite, replacing fortune with necessity. He replaces an ethic of pleasure with one of the course of Nature, which would require contemplation. He replaces an evil spirit, as the answer to what is most harmful, with vice. In answer to what is most helpful, Thales answers virtue instead of God. The Ethiopian has no conception of ethics, only comprehending good and bad as forces acting from without. Virtue and vice are the terms which govern human choice.

Cleodorus then asks, what is the difference between answering questions such as these and the riddles that his daughter, Eumetis, was fond of posing, such as: "Sooth I have seen a man with fire fasten bronze on another. Could you tell me what this is?" (154b). The answer is the medical treatment of applying heated cups to parts of the body. The comparison of such riddles to the list of questions is not pursued. It is pointed out that among the ancient Greeks, even among the poets such as Homer and Hesiod, such contests of solving perplexities were popular. The reader is left to realize that the questions to which Thales gives answers are important because they do not represent riddles but are those questions to which we require answers in order to have self-knowledge and to know how to act, and that are captured in the Delphic inscriptions. The Delphic inscriptions are not riddles.

The discussion returns to the question of the best form of government. Each of the Seven, beginning with Solon, is asked to contribute an opinion on the subject of republican government. Solon says that a state is best if it perpetuates democracy in which there is equal justice, such that injured and uninjured join together to prosecute the criminal. Bias says that an excellent democracy is when the people fear the law as much as they would fear a despot. Thales says there should be economic equality among the citizens, with none being too rich or too poor. Anacharsis says in such a state what is better should be determined by virtue and what is worse by vice. In other words, conduct of the state and its citizens should be regulated by ethical norms, not by privilege, wealth, or power.

Cleobulus says that public men should dread censure more than the law. They should do right for its own sake, not because it may make them at odds with the law. Pittacus says that as bad men should not be allowed to hold office, good men should not be allowed to refuse to serve. Those who would serve should not put their private interests above those of the state. Chilon, who, as a Spartan, does not believe that the attitude of the people is more important than the law, said that the best government is to give the greatest attention to the laws themselves, not to those who talk about them. Talking about the laws can lead to heeding views beyond those that are determined by the laws. "Finally, Periander once more concluded the discussion with the decisive remark, that they all seemed to him to approve a democracy which was most like an aristocracy" (154f).

Democracy is not advocated by the Seven as a government simply reflecting the will of the people, whatever it might be. Instead, the will of the people must be shaped by the law, good leadership, and adherence to virtue. Later, in the *Republic*, Plato will see democracy as one step away from despotism. But among the Seven, as portrayed by Plutarch, democracy is conceived as a form of the rule of the best, or aristocracy. If republican democracy can be formed as an aristocracy, then Plato would likely agree with this view of the Seven. The key to this republican form of government is the wisdom that takes the form of law and the ability to apply it.

Household Economics

Diocles, the narrator, once the discussion of government had come to an end, says that it would be appropriate for the assembled to tell us how a house should be managed. He asks this because "few persons are in control of kingdoms and states, whereas we all have to do with a hearth and home" (154f). To the modern reader it may seem strange to connect politics to home economics. Aristotle makes a similar connection by following his treatise on *Politics* with that on *Economics*. Aristotle says that the sciences of politics and economics have a common subject matter, in that the city or *polis* is composed of households. "Now a city is an aggregate made up of households and land and property, self-sufficient with regard to a good life. This is clear from the fact that, if men cannot attain this end, the community is dissolved. . . . It is evident, therefore, that economics is prior in origin to politics; for its function is prior, since a household is part of a city" (*Econ* 1343a).

The family is the smallest unit of political life and the family exists as a household. Aesop immediately points out that Anacharsis is, in effect, homeless, as he lives in a wagon that he moves from one place to another. Anacharsis comments that in so doing he lives like a god, in that he is free and independent, not ruled by anyone. He chides Aesop, calling his attention to one of his own fables, that regarding the contest of the fox and the leopard over which was more ingeniously colored. The leopard noted that the judge should not consider just her appearance but also by what was inside her. This would show her to be more ingenious. Anacharsis says that Aesop thus equates what is built by carpenters and stonemasons as a home, rather than the personal qualities of a man, his wife, children, and friends. As in the case of governments, the wise men proceed to present their opinions.

Solon said that the best home is where no injustice is involved in acquiring its property, or in keeping it, or in spending it. Bias said a home is best when the head of the household maintains the same character in governing it as he does outside, in society, in following the law. This view applies the intent in law that Bias shows in his view of right government. Thales said the best home is that in which it is possible for the head of the household to have the greatest leisure. These views reflect the claim that in household management the head of the household rules as a monarch. This view is also to be found in Aristotle, who says that "the science of politics involves a number of rulers, whereas the sphere of economics is a monarchy" (1343a).

Cleobulus said the head of the household should have more who love him than fear him. Pittacus said the best household is one that has nothing superfluous and lacks nothing necessary. This is a principle of true economy—the household is a model of prudence and moderation. Chilon said a household should be like a state ruled by a king, but adds the view of Lycurgus that a state should be a democracy and that the basis for such a state is for its citizens to create a democracy in their own manner of household management. The views of all the wise men on home economics are like those they express of the best state. Their views are in accord with the general view that a good state requires good citizens. Good citizens are grounded in well-run households and families.

The assembled digress briefly from the topic of household management to comment on the wine and the fact that it needs to be better passed around. Periander drinks to Chilon in a big beaker, and Chilon drinks in the same way to Bias. The gathering has fully become a symposium or drinking party. Drinking a big beaker is in accord with Vico's description of the custom, mentioned above in Chapter 1, of drinking larger amounts of wine toward the dinner's end. Noteworthy is the fact that drinking involves a toast. The wine is not simply sipped quietly throughout the evening. Drinking these toasts leads to a discussion on the issue of becoming drunk.

For ordinary diners, the time following dinner is an opportunity to drink, perhaps even to excess. But for those who are educated and wise, the drinking is incidental. Wine assists discourse by making a friendly atmosphere. Their conversation is governed by the Muses, who, it is reported, set only a non-intoxicating bowl. It is pointed out that Solon has the wine before him but is not drinking. Mnesiphilus, an Athenian friend of Solon, comes to his defense, pointing out that both Hesiod and Homer advocate temperance in this matter of drinking toasts. In *Works and Days*, Hesiod, in a list of prohibitions that make for good conduct in various life situations, says: "do not ever put the ladle on top of the wine-bowl while people are drinking; for a baneful fate is established for this" (744). To put the ladle on the wine bowl is to encourage those drinking to serve themselves more, which is ruinous, for it has the potential to turn the evening into a drunken scene.

In the *Iliad*, Agamemnon speaks to Idomeneus, the respected commander of the contingent from Crete, and notes that he conducts himself properly both in war and at feasts. Agamemnon says that, when others drink, Idomeneus's cup stands always full, as does his own (4.262). Mnesiphilus comments: "as nearly as I can make out, among the men of olden time the practice of drinking healths was not in vogue, since each man drank one 'goblet,' as Homer has said" (156e). It is then pointed out that this careful manner of consuming wine is said to be practiced by Zeus, who poured out wine for the gods only in measured quantity. Brillat-Savarin, in his principles of the dinner party, would agree with these ancient practices. As discussed in Chapter 1 above, it was his concern that everyone go home peacefully, to enjoy a good night's sleep.

The conversation turns back to household management and to the topic of the acquisition of some measure of property. The principle of proportion that is necessary for the management of wine at a dinner party carries over to the acquisition of property. If one has a consistent character, then property is acquired in proportion to one's needs. But an imprudent person acquires property this way and that, never able to know what is truly needed. This does not mean that everyone should have the same amount of property. In imitation of the law, Cleobulus holds, property should be acquired according to what is fitting, reasonable, and suitable to a given household and its members. The law is not simply applied uncritically. Justice requires the law to be adjusted to particular circumstances.

The sense of proportion as the basis of prudent living takes the conversation to the issue of simplicity and frugality in cooking and eating and in the promotion of health. Periander says that he believes that the earliest form of food was "inexpensive and self-propagated foods, mallow and asphodel [two types of European, perennial herbs], whose plainness and simplicity is most likely that Hesiod recommends to us" (158a). Diet is connected to medicine. The taking of herbs as part of diet is analogous to the modern incorporation of vitamins as part of one's daily meals. Solon then says: "For it is plain that the next best thing to the greatest and highest of all good is to require the minimum amount of food; or is it not the general opinion that the greatest good is to require no food at all?" (158c).

Cleodorus responds, vigorously arguing that the acquisition, preparation, and eating of food are the center of hearth and home. To reduce diet to nothing more than a form of preventive medicine is to do away with "the most humane and the first acts of communion between man and man; rather is all real living abolished, if so be that living is a spending of time by man which involves carrying a series of activities, most of which are called for by the need for food and its procurement" (158d). To eliminate dining and eating well is to deny a pleasure that is natural to the human condition. He says: "Let it be granted that there exist some superior pleasures for the soul to enjoy, yet it is not possible to discover a way for the body to attain a pleasure more justifiable than that which comes from eating and drinking, and this is a fact which no man can have failed to observe" (158f). It is then pointed out that to have no need of food is to have no need of a body, for it is the body—not the soul— that requires us to need food.

Solon comes forward to argue a strong, Stoic position, that the dependence on food is the great impediment to the self-sufficiency that should be desired and is proper to the soul. He argues that food makes us dependent on the world. Anything in nature may become food for another. Solon holds that the solution to our dependence upon food is not vegetarianism. He says: "to refrain entirely from eating meat, as they record of Orpheus of old, is rather a quibble than a way of avoiding wrong in regard to food" (159c). Thus to eat only plants and not animate beings does not avoid the corruption of our involvement with bodily existence. He says: "Indeed, in the case of most people, one can see that their soul is absolutely confined in the darkness of the body as in a mill, making its endless rounds in its concern over its need for food" (159d). He points out that now that those assembled have eaten, and the tables have been removed, they are able to spend time in conversation. They are free to exercise that which is distinctly human. At least for now they are not enslaved to food, and hence to the body.

Why should we not attempt to achieve this state of freedom throughout our whole life? To regard food and all that is needed to consume it, as the key to the human is to put the body before the soul. Solon says: "The fact is that food is taken as a remedy for hunger, and all those who use food in a prescribed way are said to be giving themselves treatment, not with the thought that they are doing something pleasant and grateful, but that this is necessary to comply with Nature's imperative demand" (160a). It can be argued that food is just as much a cause of pain as of pleasure. In fact, food can cause disease and lead even to death. The gods, as immortals, do not live by food. The divine element in human beings does not require food for its cultivation. To have minimum involvement with food is to allow the soul a new freedom. This Stoic argument for the independence from food implicitly would advocate independence from the need for property or external goods in any sense. If there are no such needs, there is no need for an individual to maintain a household. It is an extreme form of Stoicism, and even the Cynic form of life as followed by Diogenes of Sinope.

On the Soul

Toward the conclusion of Plutarch's essay, the tale is related of Arion, the famous harp player from Lesbos, and inventor of dithyrambic poetry, being saved by dolphins from drowning. Arion, encouraged by a letter he received from Periander, resolved to leave Italy for Corinth, and embarked, therefore, on a Corinthian merchant vessel. He learned while on board that the sailors planned to kill him. With no means of escape, he decided to adorn himself in the elaborate attire he wore for competitions, so that it could serve as a shroud. He placed himself on the bulwark, at the stern, and proceeded to sing one of his songs—an ode to Pythian Apollo—as the ship approached the Peloponnesus. To avoid the murderous attack of the sailors, he threw himself into the sea. But before his body was submerged, he realized that he was surrounded by many dolphins. The sea was calm and the night clear, and the dolphins bore him safely to the shore. Arion, unable to explain to himself why such a rescue had occurred, "realized that his rescue had been guided by God's hand" (162a).

The tale of Arion's rescue is followed by another tale, in which the body of Hesiod was taken up by a company of dolphins, and another tale, in which a local hero of Lesbos had been borne there, through the sea, by dolphins. Comments are made on how humane dolphins are, and how they are attracted by the sound of flutes and human song. These tales are taken as reports of actual incidents. The question is why such things should happen, as there seems no empirical explanation for them. Anacharsis then says that Thales has set forth an excellent hypothesis—that the cause of such events is divine and not material.

Thales' explanation is "that soul exists in all the most dominant and most important parts of the universe, there is no proper ground for wonder that the most excellent things are brought to pass by the will of God" (163e). God as mind or spirit is in the world as the soul is in the human body. Thus there is no reason to wonder, since the ultimate cause is divine; the world is not simply a process of material causes. Anacharsis, following Thales, says: "For the body is the soul's instrument, and the soul is God's instrument; and just as the body has many movements of its own, but the most, and most excellent, from the soul, so the soul performs some actions by its own instinct, but others it yields itself to God's use for Him to direct it and turn it in whatsoever course He may desire, since it is the most adaptable of all instruments" (163e). God, he says, makes use of any living creatures to accomplish his purposes. Hence the dolphins are agents of the divine.

Thales and Solon are the two of the seven wise men who became widely known for their doctrines. Thales is traditionally recognized as the first philosopher, and is known for his cosmology and metaphysics. Aristotle, in his *Metaphysics*, asserts that "Thales, the founder of this sort of philosophy [i.e., the one that asserts that things derive from one or more principles that serve as their substrate]."[2] Engagement in politics is attributed to Thales, according to Diogenes Laertius: "After having engaged in politics, he devoted himself to the observation of nature. [. . .] And he was the first to speak about nature as well, according to some people."[3] Diogenes further claims that to Thales "belongs the saying 'Know yourself,' which Antisthenes in his *Successions* attributes to Phemonoë saying that Chilon appropriated it for himself."[4] Cicero, in *On the Nature of the Gods*, says: "For Thales of Miletus, who was the first to investigate these matters, said that water is the beginning of things, but that god is the intelligence capable of making all things out of water."[5] This view of the world having within it a divine intelligence, is the cosmology needed to justify Thales' interpretation that the dolphins can be regarded as agents assigned to carry out the god's purpose.

Of the Seven, Solon is the chief figure of ethical wisdom. In his life of Solon Plutarch says: "In philosophy, he cultivated chiefly the domain of political ethics, like most of the wise men of the time. . . . And in general, it would seem that Thales was the only wise man of the time who carried his speculations beyond the realm of the practical; the rest got the name of wisdom from their excellence as statesmen" (*Lives*, "Solon" 3.4–5). Of the Seven Sages, Vico associates Solon most closely with the Delphic "Know thyself": "Hence Solon was made the author of that celebrated saying 'Know thyself,' which because of the great civil utility it had for the Athenian people, was inscribed in all the public places of the city. Later the learned preferred to regard it as having been intended for what in fact it is, a great counsel respecting metaphysical and moral things, and because of it Solon was reputed a sage in esoteric wisdom and made prince of the Seven Sages of Greece."[6] Solon the lawgiver, on Vico's view, formulates or at least endorses the famous inscription as a device to promote Athenian democracy, and it later takes on the status of a moral precept, to be connected to that of "Nothing overmuch."

Although both Thales and Solon are said to be the source of the two famous precepts on the temple at Delphi—*gnothi seauton* and *mēden agan*—we find at the end of Plutarch's essay a different ascription, given by Chersias the poet, who is said to have been present when the building was consecrated. Chersias says he wishes to know what the wise men say the precepts mean. Pittacus replies that their meaning is already present in the stories of Aesop. They are, then, like the advice given in the conclusions of Aesop's stories. There is added, to the two famous precepts, a third: "Give a pledge, and mischief attends" (164b). Chersias says this precept has kept many from marrying and even from trusting.

Attention is turned to the source of the famous two precepts. Aesop says Chersias in fact claims that Homer is their inventor. The source of "Know thyself" is the eleventh book of the *Iliad*, when Hector attacked the other warriors when the Trojans were being driven in rout, but Hector "knew himself" because he attacked the others but avoided a conflict with Ajax (11.542). Knowing the extent of his abilities and his position in this situation caused Hector to act prudently. The source of "Nothing overmuch" is the precept that underlies the statement of Odysseus to Diomedes in the tenth book of the *Iliad*, when he has chosen Diomedes to be his comrade-in-arms. Odysseus says not to praise or blame him too much (10.249).

Chersias also claims Homer to be the source of the third precept, regarding the problematic nature of subscribing to pledges. He cites the line in the *Odyssey* in which it is said that pledges are worthless when made by worthless people (8.351) and Zeus's pledge, in the *Iliad*, when he was fooled regarding the birth of Heracles (19.91–131). The existence of this third precept is unexpected. It is thought that the Temple of Apollo likely had more inscriptions than the famous two that survive, but the reader will likely never have heard of this third precept. An inscription that is regarded as a possible third precept is the *E* (epsilon, the fifth letter of the Greek alphabet) at Delphi. It is the word for the second person singular of the verb "to be" or "thou art." One of Plutarch's best-known essays in the *Moralia* is *The E at Delphi* (384c–394b). Much is made of it, as a third precept, by Pico della Mirandola, in his *Oration on the Dignity of Man*. Pico endorses the seventh meaning of the *E* that Plutarch gives, to indicate that the god is an eternal being.[7] However, no mention is made of the *E* as a third precept in *The Dinner of the Seven Wise Men*.

After Chersias has spoken, Solon announces that the evening should be brought to a close, quoting the wisdom of

Homer: "Night-time advances apace; 'tis well to pay heed to night-time" (164d; *Il.* 7.282 and 293). In this passage, Hector and Ajax agree to fight another day and to obey the arrival of night. The Seven may put aside their arguments and advice for another time. Solon suggests a libation be offered to the Muses and to Poseidon and his wife, Amphitrite, in order to bring the evening to an end. To offer a libation to the Muses is appropriate, since they represent the arts of humanity that guide conversation, and in addition are the retinue of Apollo. It is curious to offer a libation to Poseidon, the brother of Zeus. Perhaps Plutarch intends a play on the first syllable of Poseidon's name—*posis* (a drinking, a draught)—as this part of the dinner party has been a symposium, or drinking party.

A dinner party proper has two parts—that in which the courses of food are served, and the conversation, that begins during these courses and continues after the dining. In such a dinner, the love of food and the love of wisdom are combined, especially if the diners are learned. In the case of the dinner of the seven wise men, the after-dinner conversation becomes a symposium. In Plutarch's essay portraying the dinner, we are told little of the food, except that the dishes served were not elaborate and were unaccompanied by any special entertainment. The purpose of the dinner was to bring these learned figures together, not only to celebrate the Delphic inscriptions, but to learn their ideas that are the foundation of Greek culture. They are the teachers of the Greeks, the successors to the original wisdom of Homer and Hesiod.

The dinner of the seven wise men as Plutarch creates it stands in contrast to the relation of Athenaeus. Those assembled in the banquet of Athenaeus speak at length on food and its various types and express views on the art of living well, only now and then discussing philosophical or political ideas. The Seven speak as philosophers, not as diners. The learned banqueters speak philosophically and philologically but do so as gourmets. These two ancient accounts of dining set a standard from which any modern dinner party can find suggestions and inspiration. They deserve our attention in our roles of hosts and guests.

Chapter 3

The Learned Banqueters

> Given the opportunity at table,
> one should philosophize in an
> appropriate way, so that the
> mixing bowl of the liquid made
> for happiness is tempered by
> the influence not just of the
> Nymphs but of the Muses.
>
> Macrobius, *Saturnalia*, Book 7

Dining, Drinking, and Discourse

The fifteen books of *The Learned Banqueters of Athenaeus of Naucratis* occupy eight volumes of the Loeb Classical Library edition. This is one volume more than the Loeb edition of Augustine's great work, *The City of God against the Pagans*. It is Athenaeus's only extant work. Athenaeus cites 1,250 authors; he gives the titles of more than 1,000 plays, and quotes more than 10,000 lines of verse. These citations make the work one of the most important sources in later antiquity. The banquet is a series of dinner parties taking place over several days. Unlike Plutarch's essay on *The Dinner of the Seven Wise Men*, in which we learn little of the dinner itself, in Athenaeus's work there are wide-ranging comments on foodstuffs and wines, as well as on topics in philosophy, literature, law, medicine, and other subjects. The books of Athenaeus are quoted in some modern cookbooks that have a historical interest and his name is kept alive in this regard.[1] There is a brief, and rather strange, entry in the *Larousse Gastronomique* identifying Athenaeus, with a single comment noting that in his work "there are several passages relating to flowers and fruit and their various uses, both practical and pleasurable."[2]

Athenaeus's work is not only long, it is rambling and unstructured, a jumble of material. The books are a great series of digressions in which the digressions are the text itself. The translator of the Loeb volumes, S. Douglas Olson, says that the work functions on two narrative levels: "The first (which frames the second) is a conversation between Timocrates, who has heard rumors of a brilliant dinner party and would like to learn more, and a character named Athenaeus, who was present at the events in question." Timocrates acts as Athenaeus's interlocutor. There is a second level that "is an account of the banquet itself, and although the character of Athenaeus mostly quotes the other guests directly, he also describes in his own words what was served, how the company reacted to their companions' speeches, and the like."[3]

The host of the banquet is Larensius of Rome, who not only is responsible for the venue of the banquet but also is praised for the excellence of his library. One is reminded here of the availability of a library that Vico notes in his account of Roman banquets, mentioned in Chapter 1, above. Larensius, after being introduced, recedes into the background, unlike Periander, the host of the dinner of the seven wise men, who actively presents his views along with the seven. A dominant figure in Athenaeus's text is the grammarian Ulpian of Tyre, who is not to be confused with the famous Ulpianus the jurisconsult, quoted widely by the compilers of *Justinian's Digest*. Ulpian has as his intellectual rival in the conversation the Cynic philosopher Theodorus, who is called Cynulcus throughout. As Olson remarks in the introduction to the translation: "both men are characterized primarily via the brief remarks that begin and end their speeches; otherwise they serve as little more than vehicles for long strings of quotations, anecdotes, and catalogues."[4] As mentioned above in Chapter 1, the participants also include four philosophers, four physicians, three musicians, eight grammarians, and a lexicographer.

Given the size of the work and that its narrative is more a compilation than a systematic speech, one wonders if anyone really reads Athenaeus's text from beginning to end. Its fifteen books are daunting and do not easily hold the reader's attention. Yet it is a classic for thinking through the idea of dining. My intention in what follows is to state something of the essence of each book, so that it may be of service for anyone to know to some extent what is in the work. In so doing my guiding question is: What can be learned from the learned banqueters regarding dining, drinking, and discourse?

Book 1: Early Meals

Athenaeus says that this banquet brings together "the greatest experts in every field of knowledge" (1.1a). It is a banquet of many experts in particular facts and areas of knowledge, in contrast to the *Dinner of the Seven Wise Men*, who are wise in philosophical questions concerning the order of nature, ruling of the State, and the human psyche. As mentioned in Chapter 2, they say little about the food eaten except to discuss the general question of human nourishment. In contrast, Athenaeus announces he "omits no one's finest sayings; for he included fish in his book, and the ways they are prepared and the derivations of their names, as well as every sort of vegetable, animals of every kind, and authors of historical works, poets, and philosophers. He also described musical instruments, a million types of jokes, different styles of drinking cups, the wealth of kings, huge ships—and so many other items that I could not easily mention them all" (1.1a–b). The Seven Sages, besides citing each other, refer mostly to Homer. Homer also plays a role in Athenaeus's account.

The dinner party that Athenaeus presents follows the principle that such an event is of two parts—the food served and the conversation that accompanies it and succeeds it. Included in the conversation is the specific discussion of types of food and types of wine as well as topics of all sorts. The feast of food is also a "delightful feast of words" (1.1b). Although Athenaeus says: "The account is arranged to imitate the extravagance of the dinner party, and the book's structure reflects how the dinner was organized" (1.1b). The reader must just go with what is said without wondering why it is said at this or that particular point, taking what is said to be simply of intrinsic interest.

Athenaeus quotes from a poem in epic verse by Archastratus of Syracuse, advocating that: "Everyone should dine at a single table set for an elegant meal" (1.4e). At such a meal, Archastratus says, the number of guests should be three or four and at any rate not more than five. There is discussion of whether to eat sitting at a table or reclining on couches: "The heroes sit at their banquets rather than reclining" (1.17f). It is pointed out that to lie down before dinner is served has no point because one cannot fall asleep (1.23d).

It is also said that "Banqueters in Homer did not take the leftovers home, but ate as much as they wanted and left the rest behind with their hosts" (1.13a). This is in contrast to Vico's claim, regarding the dinners of the Romans, to which the guests brought napkins in which to take home tidbits (as discussed in Chapter 1, above). It is also stated that in Homer each diner had a bread-basket and a wine goblet (1.13d). There is mention of the taking of baths before dinner, a custom also of the Romans. The ancient heroes ate all types of meat as well as fish and also vegetables (1.24e). There is discussion of the merits of white wine versus red, and of types of wine generally (1.32c).

Book 2: Water, Wine, and Appetizers

Wine is essential to the symposium that follows a dinner but it is also present at the beginning of a meal. This presence of wine at the beginning of a meal is reflected in the service of a traditional Italian *trattoria*. When one is seated, bread is immediately brought and the diners are asked whether they wish white or red wine. Before drinking it is customary for the diners to say, "Salute," in effect toasting each other. This toast is a vestige of drinking to the gods. Athenaeus reports: "The epic poet Panyasis assigns the first round of drinks to the Graces, the Seasons, and Dionysus; the second to Aphrodite and Dionysus again; but the third to Outrage and Folly" (2.36d). Dining itself is connected to sacrifice: "A sacrifice leads to a feast, and a feast leads to drinking" (2.36c–d). The pouring of a libation is symbolic of a sacrifice. The meal is an extension of the sacrifice. Athenaeus says: "Aristotle says that the verb *methuō* ("be drunk") refers to the fact that one consumes wine *meta to thuein* ("after making sacrifice") (2.40d).

Since wine is an essential part of dining, there is concern among the ancient authors regarding drunkenness. This concern supports the universal practice among the Greeks to mix water with wine. "Philochorus says that Amphictyon the king of Athens learned how to mix wine from Dionysus and was the first person to do this" (2.38c). There is also much discussion of the need also to drink water in and of itself for health as well as to bathe before meals. "One should avoid thick perfumes and drink water that appears thin and transparent, and that is in fact light in weight and contains no sediment" (2.46b). There is much discussion of types of water and the merits of the sources of the best water. This discussion is reminiscent of the various mineral waters available today, and of the second question asked of the diners in a traditional *trattoria*, regarding which type of water they might prefer, *gassata* or *non-gassata* (carbonated or non-carbonated).

Following the discussion of wine and water, Athenaeus says: "It was the custom at dinner parties for the host to be offered a writing tablet with a list of the dishes when he lay down, so that he would know what food the cook was going to serve" (2.49d). This tablet is the menu or *listino*. The items discussed, which range from radishes, saltfish, asparagus, sausages, barley-cakes, hyacinth bulbs, oysters, snails, thrushes, partridges, hares, eggs, cucumbers, melons, lettuce, and so forth are a combination of vegetables, seafood, fowl, and meats. Their merits and digestion are discussed at length. These appetizers are presumably now served to Larensius's guests. The principle this offering embodies is that a wide variety of small and varied dishes are appropriate for the appetizer course.

Book 3: The Fish Course and the Boiled Course

Book 3 begins with the assertion that: "The grammarian Callimachus used to say that a big book is equivalent to a big evil" (3.72a). Athenaeus makes no comment on this quotation but proceeds immediately to continue his discussion of foodstuffs. He is producing as big a book as one can imagine and apparently cannot help himself but to do so.

The text moves to a discussion of the greatness of figs. Magnus says: "the fig-tree, my friends, was mankind's guide to the refined way of life" (3.74d). He comments on its status among the Athenians and claims that it was the first domesticated food to be discovered. Pages of quotations follow, describing and praising figs. We learn that: "Heracleides of Tarentum in his *Symposium* raises the question of whether one ought to consume warm water or cold water after eating figs" (3.79e). One view is that warm water breaks down their structure and makes them more digestable but that cold water makes them more firm in the stomach. Another view is that the weight of the cold water pushes the figs downward and thus aids with digestion. The discussion of figs is followed by one on citron, and whether the ancients mentioned it anywhere (3.83a). It is pointed out that the Romans refer to citron as *kitros* or *citrus* (3.85c).

But "Immediately after the items described above, large quantities of oysters and other shellfish were brought in on separate platters" (3.85c). These include scallops, barnacles, black conch and white conch, octopus, squid, crayfish, mussels, shrimp, clams, and whelks. This service is in effect a fish course, presented after the appetizer. There is much discussion of each of these, including their digestibility. Moving from appetizer to a first course of fish is to be found today, especially in French meals, although in this case the fish course is all shellfish. In a French meal it might more commonly be a poached fish such as a turbot or a lightly sautéed fillet of sole.

"After this, platters were carried around loaded with many types of boiled meat: feet, heads, ears, jawbones, and also tripe, intestines, and tongues, as is customary in what are called the boil-shops in Alexandria" (3.94.c). This boiled course corresponds to the course following the *antipasto* (or first course) in the order of Florentine dining in the sixteenth century, as described by Bugialli: "The second course was the boiled course. This never varied, whether the third course was fried dishes or roasted dishes."[5] There was no fish course preceding it. In the Florentine meal of today the pasta course occupies the place of the boiled course. It is a kind of boiled course, as the pasta is prepared by boiling.

There are two general comments of note. One is the observation that diners without education put a premium on having entertainment while drinking wine after dinner, because, lacking learning, they also lack conversation (3.97a–b). Another decries the "ignorance of today's cooks," who mix various things together thinking they are inventive but in fact do not know how to prepare or combine food harmoniously (3.102e–103a). This principle, when understood, should prevent the contemporary practice of "stacked food," and of thinking that the basis of cooking is individual invention rather than the perfection of tradition.

Book 4: A Wedding Dinner, Spartan Meals

Book 4 begins with a description of a wedding dinner in Macedon, at which silver and gold bowls and platters were employed, and given to the guests. After some first plates were served and some entertainment: "Then a fortune was served instead of dinner: a silver platter covered with heavy goldplate, and large enough to hold a huge roast piglet lying on its back and displaying its belly, which was full of many delicious items; for inside it were roast thrushes, ducks, and an immense quantity of warblers, as well pea soup poured over hard-boiled eggs, as well as oysters and scallops" (4.129b). The guests were given an assortment of these items, along with the platters. Then they were given a piping hot kid, along with the platter it was on, accompanied by gold spoons. The custom of giving guests some form of gift at such special occasions persists in some cultures today, although not so extravagant.

In contrast to such dining there is a description of Spartan meals eaten at military men's messes. "The dinner is initially served to each man separately, and nothing is shared with anyone else. Then there is a barley-cake as large as each of them wants; and, moreover, a cup is set beside each man to drink whenever he wishes" (4.141b). Everyone is given some stewed pork and broth from the meat "and perhaps an olive, some cheese, or a fig, or if they are given something extra, a fish, a hare, a ring-dove, or the like" (4.141c). It is said they eat these meals quickly. But: "The Spartans later abandoned a way of life as austere as this and drifted into luxury" (4.141f).

The book offers a catalogue of how meals are composed and eaten by various ancient peoples. In regard to dining among the Parthians, a strange practice is described: "The man referred to as the king's 'friend' does not share his food, but sits on the ground below the king, who lies on a high couch, and eats whatever is thrown to him like a dog. Often for one reason or another he is dragged away from his dinner on the ground and beaten with rods or whips to which knucklebones have been attached" (4.152f). The man then returns to the dinner to worship the king as his benefactor. One thinks of the court custom of having a taster who tries the king's food to determine that it is not poisoned. The taster has a clear-cut, practical role. The king's "friend," in this case, has no such role except to demonstrate to others the extent of the king's power.

The book ends with some remarks on the enjoyable sounds made by a hydraulic organ and the origin of string and wind musical instruments.

Book 5: The Learned Speech of Masurius on Symposia

Nearly all of Book 5 is a speech of Masurius on symposia, beginning with "Homeric symposia." Types of food or dishes eaten are not discussed, in favor of advocating the importance of symposia and its involvement with philosophy. Masurius is "a legal scholar who paid serious attention to learning of every sort, an extraordinary poet, and a man second to none in other sorts of culture, who had shown great eagerness for getting a comprehensive education" (1.1c).

Masurius regards the high purpose of dinners to be the occasions for symposia. Symposia are characterized as exchanges of learning. He says: "The lawgivers were anticipating today's dinner parties when they mandated meals organized by tribes and communities, as well as cult-dinners, phratry-dinners, and also those referred to as *orgeōnika* [dinners organized by a religious association]" (5.185c). By connecting symposia with passages in Homer, Masurius is associating symposia with Greek culture itself. He says: "Homer teaches us what we ought to do before we feast, which is to offer the gods first fruits of the food" (5.179b). The act of eating as well as that of drinking that occupies the symposium that follows the dinner affords connection to the gods. They are not simply biological acts. Masurius says: "Plato retains these elements in his symposium; after they had dinner, he says, they made libations and sang a paean to the god, giving him his customary honors [see *Smp.* 176a]" (5.179d).

Having related views of symposia and dinners derived from Homer which are prudent and intelligent, Masurius asks: "What name, then, shall we use, my friends, for the symposium given by Antiochus, who was referred to as Epiphanes, but whose actions earned him the title Epimanes ('the Madman')?" (5.193d). He then describes at great length a festival and parade that involved thousands of marchers and scores of various types of animals, leading to an opulently decorated venue and elaborately served dinner, as well as an account of a magnificent ship.

This so-called symposium is a fantastic event, but without any intellectual meaning. It is followed by a critical analysis of symposia, involving various ancient philosophers. Masurius displays his learning in a series of errors he exposes in the details of philosopher's texts, including Plato's *Symposium.* Masurius concludes that: "The philosophers thus lie about everything and fail to realize that much of what they write is full of anachronisms" (5.216c).

Book 6: Parasites, Flatterers, and Slaves

Book 6 opens with the speaker reaffirming that he is relating a true account of the learned banqueters' conversation and not inventing odd fictions. Among others, he quotes the comic poet Timocles: "Listen, mister, and see if what I say makes sense to you" (6.223b). Although Timocles is speaking about tragedy, the claim is presented as also applying to the narration herein.

Slaves enter the room, bearing silver platters with an array of saltwater and freshwater fish. This provokes a long discourse on types of fish, as well as remarks on the use of silver vessels at dinner parties in terms of where their use is to be found at such parties. It is reported that: "The first silver and gold dedications in Delphi were made by Gyges, king of Lydia" (6.231e).

The meaning and role of "parasite" is raised. Plutarch is cited as holding that: "Long ago 'parasite' was a sacred, holy term" (6.234d). Polemon is quoted as saying: "'Parasite' is today a disreputable term, but among the ancients I find that the parasite was sacred and resembled an invited guest at a meal" (6.234e). Parasites are known to practice flattery and it is said that there can be two kinds of parasites, one that is a common type seen in comedies and another who is attached to satraps (governors of provinces) and generals (6.237b–c). Both are said to excel in flattery.

A parasite (*parasites*) is one who frequents the table of the rich and may, in fact, live generally at another's expense. The claim that "parasite" was originally a noble term may stem from its use to designate a class of assistants in ancient Greek religious rites who dined with the priests following a sacrifice. The discussion of parasites turns into a general discussion of flattery in which it is affirmed that: "The Athenian people were notorious for their use of flattery" (6.252f). Many examples of flattery are produced, and we are told: "From all these examples, my friends, one can see how much trouble flattery causes in our lives" (6.260a).

From the difficulties of flatterers the conversation drifts into the difficulties of owning slaves. It is pointed out that slaves were employed by the Greeks to do all kinds of tasks, including preparing and serving dinners. As these remarks come to a close, it is once again said that these reminiscences have gone on long enough and they are thus concluded.

Book 7: Types of Fish

Book 7 begins with the announcement that the dinner is now coming to an end. It closes with the speaker saying that he will retire for the night, the entire day having been used up by the discussions of Books 6 and 7.

The conversation turns to the subject of fish broached at the beginning of Book 6. The speaker says: "I will recall for you what the learned banqueters said about each fish; because they all contributed to the discussion of the subject from their books" (7.277b–c). Page after page of quotations follow, concerning all conceivable types of fish. There is attention to what these fish are like to eat, but much of the discussion is simply biological description.

For example, it is reported of eels that they easily suffocate in muddy water and that: "The eel farmers report that they feed at night and lie motionless in the muck during the day, and generally live for eight years" (7.298e). It is said that the rockfish, according to Aristotle: "is solitary, carnivorous, and jagged-toothed; black in color; and has disproportionately large eyes and a white, triangular heart" (7.301c). It is said, also according to Aristotle, that: "Tuna and swordfish behave insanely in late summer; because at that time they both carry near their fins something that resembles a small worm, known as the *oistros*, which is like a scorpion, but the size of a spider" (7.302b).

Such descriptions are not directed to the types of fish as food—how to prepare them or how they taste—but as enumerations of their natural characteristics. At some points, however, there are comments interspersed concerning whether a certain fish is good to eat. For example, Archestratus is quoted: "But when you come to Byzantium, buy a swordfish steak, the very backbone section of the tail" (7.314e–f). And: "Mithaecus says in the *Art of Cooking*: After you gut a *tainia* and remove its head, wash it off and cut it into steaks, and pour cheese and olive oil over it" (7.326a). Since fish is not ordinarily prepared with cheese, this is an interesting culinary concept, but not further developed.

Although octopus is widely eaten even today, it is discussed at length in biological terms, relying on Aristotle, among other writers, explaining that: "The octopus mates in the winter and bears its young in the spring. It retreats into a burrow for about two months" (7.317d).

Book 7 is an aquatic encyclopedia, exposited by the banqueters largely for its own sake and not convincing as a dinner conversation. It seems a digression from the narrative, but that, as stated earlier, is itself a series of digressions.

Book 8: More Fish and Some Gluttons

Book 8 begins by adding to the discussion of fish that occupied Book 7. It is reported that Cynulcus, the Cynic philosopher, was irritated because this lengthy aquatic discussion had caused the serving of dinner to be deferred. It is immediately deferred even more because the philosopher, Democritus of Nicomedia, insists that he needs: "to add a few more fish to our shopping list" (8.331c). Thus the encyclopedia of fish goes on, including the remark: "you have thrown us to the fish rather than the other way around" (8.335a), that is to say, by making such long speeches about fish we have been unable to eat any.

The continuing discussion of fish leads to a discussion of gluttons and gluttony: "The word *opsophagos* ('glutton') is used, my friends, as is *opsophagein* ('to be a glutton')" (8.345f). Various gluttons are named and passages on gluttony are quoted. We are not told why gluttony becomes a topic mixed with the discussion of fish. Fish seems a rather light food, not too filling, whereas gluttony seems more to be associated with consuming whole legs of lamb or great quantities of roasts, perhaps also great numbers of oysters. This sense of gluttony reminds one of scenes of meals of Rabelaisian proportions. Democritus relates an example of the Syrian queen, Gatis, who: "was such a glutton that she announced that no one was to eat fish except (*ater*) Gatis" (8.346c). Her subjects were ordered to bring all fish to her to eat. The topic of gluttony itself is part of what in fact is a gluttony of words. The discussion of fish is a mental gluttony, a discussion continued almost for its own sake.

The book ends with the claim that human beings originally came from the sea: "Since this treatise too has come to an end, my friend Timocrates, it is appropriate for me to conclude my speech at this point, so that no one believes that I was ever a fish [and am thus overly interested in them], as Empedocles was. For the scientist says: 'Because before this I was a boy, a girl, a bush, a bird, and an *ellopos* fish leaping out of the sea'" (8.365e). This is a line concerning the transmigrations of living beings, from the poems of Empedocles.[6] Empedocles's statement is directed to the origin of human beings as distinct from gods, and is not meant as a claim concerning his own personal origin. This sense of origin is in contrast to the apotheosis of Empedocles at the end of his life, as related by Heraclides of Pontus.[7]

Book 9: Dinner Resumes

Book 9 begins with a quotation from the fourth book of the *Odyssey*, in which Menelaus says: "Let us think once again of our dinner, and let them pour water over our hands; and beginning at dawn there will be stories (*Od*.4.213–14)" (9.366a). The original Greek is quoted precisely, but the translation is somewhat misleading. The "stories" at dawn means that Menelaus will have opportunity to have a full conversation with Telemachus. Here the quotation is used as a preface, to resume the description of the foods served at dinner.

It is then reported that hams were served, and Ulpian, the grammarian, intervenes to question several terms associated with ham and the sauce with which it is served. He questions whether mustard should be called *napu* or *sinapu*. This is an example of the terminological interjections of Ulpian that run throughout all fifteen books. Sauces for seafood are mentioned, and Ulpian says: "I see that fermented fish-sauce has been mixed with the vinegar, and I know that nowadays some residents of the Black Sea region manufacture a vinegar-and-fermented-fish sauce specifically as such" (9.366c). This sauce is likely a version of the famous *garum* that appears in the cookbook of Apicius.

After some discussion and quotations concerning types of ham and sauces, Athenaeus announces: "Immediately after this, many different types of food were served; I will describe only those that deserve special mention" (9.368f). What follows are accounts of turnips, cabbage, beets, carrots, leeks, gourds; then chickens are discussed at length. There are interesting comments on the Greek words for rooster, including the comic exchange in the *Clouds* in which Aristophanes has Socrates tell Strepsiades that *alektruaina* ("roosteress") should be used as a feminine form in contrast to the male term, *alektōr* (rooster). Athenaeus says: "It has this name because it rouses us from bed (*lektron*)" (9.374d). One is reminded of the death scene at the end of the *Phaedo*, when Socrates tells Crito to offer a cock to Asclepius, the god of healing. It is likely directed to Aristophanes, since his false portrayal of Socrates in the *Clouds* did much to shape the negative opinion of Socrates' activity held by the *hoi polloi*.

As the dinner proceeds a pig is served, stuffed with thrushes and various other birds. Geese, pheasants, partridges, quail, swans, pigeons, ducks, peacocks, larks, and ostriches were served, received with many citations and comments. Also there were suckling-pigs, hares, wild boars, and various casserole dishes combining meats and vegetables.

At one point the views of several cooks are quoted, regarding how to prepare and serve a meal. It is said that: "Organization implies wisdom everywhere, in every profession; but in ours it's almost the most important quality there is" (9.378f). The principles are expressed that various dishes must be served at just the right moment, depending upon whether they are hot, cold, or at room temperature. The meal must be properly paced, with an almost military sense of strategy.

Book 10: Athenaeus's Method

Book 10 opens and closes with quotations that are programmatic for the whole of Athenaeus's speech to Timocrates on the learned banqueters. He first quotes from the satyr play *Heracles*, by the tragic poet Astydamas: "A clever poet should supply his audience with a rich feast that resembles an elegant dinner, so everyone eats and drinks whatever he likes before he leaves, and the entertainment doesn't consist of a single course" (10.411b). Although Athenaeus's narration is not a poem, it is conceived by him in accordance with this analogy of a literary work and a banquet. At a banquet one may eat and drink whatever one wishes from a totality that is set out before the guests. Athenaeus's text presents the reader with all that can be thought and has been thought in regard to dining, considered as a feast of food and of words, of the distinctively human act of eating and of knowing (*homo sapiens*).

The theme of Book 10, at least in part, is the gluttony of Heracles (Roman, Hercules). Athenaeus says: "Almost every poet and prose-author makes this clear" (10.411b). Heracles is the greatest of the heroes and the greatest of eaters. Athenaeus's task is Herculean in that he must put together all that can be said concerning eating. Athenaeus concludes Book 10 by quoting Metagenes's *The Man Who Loved Sacrifices*: "I vary my plot interlude by interlude, in order to feast my audience on many novel appetizers" (10.459c).

In presenting his narration Athenaeus likens what he says to serving appetizers. The reader, like the diner, is to try one after another, finding whatever he may like in each. Athenaeus likely introduces these insights into his method at this late date in his speech because now his audience, including Timocrates, can best appreciate them, having had ongoing experience of how his thoughts appear.

Besides remarks on the gluttony of Heracles, much of Book 10 is taken up with comments on the drinking of wine and the importance of avoiding drunkenness. Thus:

"According to Plato in Book VI of the *Laws* (775b–c) drinking until you are intoxicated is not appropriate or safe anywhere except at the festivals celebrated in honor of the god who gave us wine" (10.431f). Plato's *Republic* (562c–d) is also cited, drawing an analogy between the need for moderation in the ruling of cities as for moderation in the consumption of wine by tempering the wine with sufficient water (10.444a–b). Drunkenness is gluttony in regard to wine.

Book 11: Types of Drinking Vessels

The theme of Book 11, concerning the various types of cups from which to drink, follows naturally from the discussion of wine. It opens with the statememt: "Because we had gathered on time and with considerable excitement, motivated by the drinking vessels; and while everyone was still seated, and before there had been any conversation. Ulpian said: 'In Adrastus' house, my friends, the nobles eat dinner seated'" (11.459d). The topic of cups had been announced at the end of Book 10; thus there is anticipation of this and of the drinking party that was to accompany it. Everyone is seated, but they will recline on their couches when the drinking party or symposium will begin. Ulpian remarks on the fact that nobles eat dinner seated.

Ulpian's remark recalls a passage in Book 10 concerning the Greeks in this regard: that "when they began to live a pampered, luxurious life-style, they slipped off their chairs onto couches; made relaxation and leisure their allies; and began to get drunk in a careless, sloppy way, being led into hedonism, in my opinion, by their possessions" (10.428b). The practice of sitting at table is older than reclining on couches. But the learned banqueters will follow the custom of reclining while drinking. That luxury corrupts is a claim that is held by the ancients as well as the eighteenth-century *philosophes*.

"The word [for cups, "*potēria*"] is derived from *posis* ('drink'); compare the use of *ekpōma* ('drinking vessel') by

Attic authors, who employ the verbs *hudropotein* ('to drink water') and *oinopotein* ('to drink wine')" (11.460b–c). It is also pointed out that *kulix* is a common term for a drinking cup. The discussion turns to whether the ancients used large cups when they drank and it is pointed out that the king's cup was always large. It is also pointed out that "The so-called Seven Wise Men also held drinking parties" (11.463c). Wine, it is said, offers consolation for the misery of old age. Also, "It is said that people originally drank using cow's horns; as a consequence, statues of Dionysus have horns, and many poets refer to him as a bull" (11.476a).

As might be expected, the reader is given many pages cataloging types of cups, made from various metals as well as wood, in various shapes, presented in terms of quotations from numerous ancient authors. The reader is justifiably baffled as to why the learned banqueters are so interested in what is a great quantity of minutia, accompanied by much lexical discussion. It is clear that Athenaeus is quite interested in it, but the extended discussion of these vessels contains no real ideas about dining or symposia, except for the insistence on the importance of mixing water with wine.

Book 12: Those Who Are Addicted to Luxury

The narrator, Athenaeus, opens this book with the claim that Timocrates has asked him again and again to relate accounts of individuals who were addicted to luxury, and their dissipation. Underlying his narrative is the view of the Cyrenaiac philosophical school that advocated pleasure to be the supreme good. He claims that the Cyrenaic sect originated with Socrates' friend Aristippus of Cyrene (12.544a). The remarks on the Cyrenaic school that Athenaeus makes are generally accurate to their doctrine.

Athenaeus says that for the Cyrenaics, "pleasure exists only in the individual moment" (12.544b). The memory of past pleasure or the expectation of pleasures to come are of no significance. The Good exists exclusively in the moment.

It is simply the moment that gives one pleasure. This view is a direct challenge to the Socratic claim that pleasure cannot be the Good because to pursue it is like attempting to fill a bucket with a hole in it. The bucket can never be filled. One pleasure must constantly be replaced by another. Instead of seeing this impermanence of pleasure as a defect in guiding human action, the Cyrenaics claim it to be its value. The Cyrenaics lived for the enjoyment of the moment and regarded this sense of life as natural. Pleasure was not simply the avoidance of pain but was a positive state in itself. One pleasure was regarded to be as good as another. There was no hierarchy of pleasures.

Athenaeus devotes the whole of the book to examples of the pursuit of luxury that would coincide with the Cyreniac view of pleasure. He says: "The first people to be notorious for their addition to luxury were the Persians" (12.513f). Luxury in this and succeeding instances is not especially connected to dining, but to exorbitant life styles. He says the Etruscans led lives of unheard-of luxury (12.517d). This view accords with the general historical judgment that the Etruscans were a pleasure-loving people. Athenaeus says: "Sicilian tables are notoriously luxurious" (12.518c). He names also the Sybarites and the Crotonites as committed to luxury, as well as the Iberians. He regards luxury as always eventually corrupting a people. He says the Scythians were the first to have laws that applied to everyone, and thus they created a strong society, but then they became addicted to luxury and were overwhelmed by it (12.524c).

These are some of the various peoples that Athenaeus lists, as well as various individuals. Toward the end of his narrative he says: "How much better it is, my good Timocrates, to be poor and thinner than the individuals Hermippus lists in *Cercopes* (fr.36), than to be much too rich and resemble the sea-monster in Tanagra, like the men mentioned above!" (12.551a). By implication, the position of Athenaeus appears to be some form of moderation, but one that does not deny the value of pleasure and that finds the pursuit of pleasure to be natural, if regulated by prudence.

Book 13: Matters Relating to Love

Athenaeus turns from the general topic of luxury to that of love. He says that the learned banqueters often "talked about married women as well as courtesans [*hetaerae*] . . . I will first invoke the Muse Erato, asking that I have no difficulty recalling my catalogue of erotica" (13.555b). The *hetaerae* are the class of highly cultivated women of ancient Greece separate from the class of married women or slaves. Erato is the Muse of lyric poetry, but here there is a pun on *eros*. The pun is apt, since love poetry is lyric in form. Athenaeus's reference to memory fits with Mnemosyne, or Memory, being the mother of the Muses.

Book 13, like the one before it, is a catalogue of examples of its subject. Sexual relations are pleasures that go along with those of dining, but they are presented here as natural and not a matter of dissipation, as is the addiction to luxury. Athenaeus says that: "What I have described are actual courtesans, which is to say, women capable of maintaining a friendship not based on trickery" (13.571c). Courtesans do not exploit nor are they exploited. They conduct themselves as friends. "Even today, at any rate, free women and girls refer to their friends and associates as *hetairai*" (13.571d).

Athenaeus is in favor of the role of courtesans and speaks throughout in a positive manner regarding their role. He wishes to show that courtesans are not in competition with the pursuit of philosophy. He says: "Did not this Epicurus, at any rate, have Leontion, who was notorious for being a courtesan, as his lover? Nor did she stop working as a prostitute once she began to study philosophy, and she had sex with all Epicurus' followers in the Gardens, even right before Epicurus' eyes" (13.588b). The Epicureans generally accepted *hetaerae* into their circle. Athenaeus's reference to Epicurus is significant because the doctrine of pure pleasure of the Cyrenaics historically disintegrated before the advance of the modified hedonism of Epicurus.

Athenaeus says Epicurus claims: "For I, at any rate, am unable to conceive of 'the Good' if I remove from consideration the pleasure derived from the favors of food, or from sex, or from music, or if I exclude bodily motions that are pleasant to watch" (13.546e). The purely kinetic pleasure of Aristippus must be connected to the absence of disturbance of the soul, or *ataraxia*, endorsed by the Epicurean ethic. Indeed, some form of Epicureanism appears to be the philosophical underpinning of the learned banqueters. In support of this view is the fact that Book 13 ends with an attack on the Cynic philosophy of incivility, saying that the Cynics are "foul-mouthed gluttons" willing to say or eat anything and who "live without a hearth or a home" (13.611d).

Book 14: Second Tables

This book opens with an admonition not to drink strong wine or to drink too much, a frequent theme throughout Athenaeus's narrative. These brief remarks are followed by a discussion of various forms of musical entertainment, also a theme previously encountered. Included in this discourse is the report that "Our parties also featured rhapsodes. For Larensius [the host] was more fond of Homer's poetry than anyone can imagine" (14.620b). Listening to music and to rhapsodes reciting Homer's poetry would replace conversation but also provide a basis for it. Regarding music, the comic poet Eupolis is quoted: "Music's a profound business—and a complicated one, which always presents those capable of appreciating it with something new" (14.623e). The virtues of music are discussed at length. At one point it is said: "In the old days, music encouraged bravery" (14.627a). It is also said that the Spartans go into battle accompanied by pipes and the Cretans go accompanied by the lyre (14.627d).

Then, "After Masurius completed these lengthy remarks [on music], what are referred to as the second tables were brought around for us" (14.639b). The second tables are laden with little plates of nuts, dried fruits, and savories, as well as pastries and cakes. These are referred to as *epiphorēmata*, from the verb *epidorpisasthai*, "to snack," "to eat something after dinner" (14.640f). The second table corresponds to the general principle of dessert and is regarded as a considerable expense. It is connected to a long discussion of types of cakes, mostly composed of wheat, honey, and figs. The second table can also include peacocks or partridges as well as slices of ham.

The second table may include a special dish called *muma*. "A *muma* of any sort of meat, including chicken, should be made by dicing up the soft portions of the meat; stirring them in with the entrails, the guts, and the blood; and seasoning the dish with vinegar, roasted cheese, silphium [an extinct plant used medicinally by the Greeks], cumin, fresh and dried coriander, a bulb-less onion, some nice toasted onion or poppy-seeds, raisins or honey, and seeds from an acidic pomegranate" (14.662d–e). It is pointed out that *muma* can also be made from fish, but the recipe is not provided. Exactly how *muma* would taste is a challenge to the culinary imagination, especially with the inclusion of chicken entrails and blood. Perhaps if other meat is used it is a forerunner of souse or the Pennsylvania Dutch dish, "scrapple." *Muma* would qualify as a savory in the course of the second table.

The book closes with Athenaeus saying it was now evening, and the banqueters go their separate ways.

Book 15: The Origin and Purpose of Garlands

The fifteenth book of this excessively long work presents the reader with no particular conclusion. Athenaeus begins by quoting Euripides: "If a god were to grant me the eloquent melodiousness of Nestor or Phrygian Antenor, to quote the insightful Euripides (fr.899), my friend Timocrates, I would be unable even so to recall for you what was said on every occasion at those brilliant parties, on account of both the diversity and the similarity of the ever-new topics put forward" (15.665a). Euripides' reference is to the third book of the *Iliad*, where it is said that Antenor, as well as other leaders of the Trojans, being too old for battle, became good speakers, "like cicadas that in a forest sit on a tree and pour out their lily-like voice" (*Il.*3.148–53). Athenaeus says further: "The fact is that the conversation routinely involved the order of the dishes served and the events that followed the meal, and I can recount what was said only with difficulty" (15.665a).

Athenaeus's narration is like the voice of the cicadas, as it goes on and on and we cannot cease listening. One is reminded of the passage in Plato's *Phaedrus*, in which the cicadas, who once were human beings, after their brief lives report to the Muses on who is leading a philosophical life (259c). Athenaeus reports to Timocrates, and hence to us, the philosophical nature of the human activity of dining. Given the length of his narrative, it is difficult to believe he has left much of anything out. His narrative is a mental magnet that draws everything toward itself.

Most of this final book is a discussion of the practice of making and wearing garlands. Athenaeus gives a physiological account of the origin of garlands. They originated as a cure for the headaches that resulted from too much drinking at dinner parties: "For when someone's head hurt, according to Andreas, he applied pressure to it and got relief, and he thus discovered that wrapping cures a headache. At their drinking parties, therefore, they used this form of assistance and began to bind the participants' heads" (15.675d).

There is a discussion of the types of garlands best suited for this purpose, such as ivy, myrtle, roses, laurel, or even marjoram. Since garlands have a pleasant smell, the discussion proceeds to the use of perfumes. Garlands and perfumes add to the atmosphere of dinner parties. "Garlands and perfume used to be brought into the party just before the second table, as Nicostratus establishes in *Falsely Tattooed* (fr.27), in the following passage: 'You! Get the second table ready! Put all kinds of snacks on it! And get perfume, garlands, frankincense, and a pipe-girl'" (15.685c–d).

The work ends with a complicated statement, the most philosophical thing said in the entire fifteen books. "The preceding, my dearest Timocrates, were not the witty remarks of Plato's young and handsome Socrates, but the earnest conversation pursued by the learned banqueters. For to quote Dionysius Chalcous, 'What is finer, as we begin or end, than what we desire most?'" (15.702c). Athenaeus's reference is to the second letter of Plato, in which he says nothing of his doctrine has ever been written down, nor should any true doctrine be written down. It is best committed to memory. Plato says: "There is no writing of Plato's, nor will there ever be; those that are now called so come from an idealized and youthful Socrates. Farewell and heed my warning; read this letter again and again, then burn it" (*Ep* 2.314c; see also 7.341c).

What is the intention of Athenaeus in this final reflection on his work? He has begun the work by affirming that it is a first-hand report (1.1f). Thus it is a true account of what occurred. It is, however, a written account. The reader or listener, including Timocrates, must realize that the meaning of what is said cannot be written down. All real philosophy is esoteric, beyond speech, even if pursued at the level of the Greek orators, those whom, Athenaeus says, are his models.

The line from Dionysius Chalcous, a poet of the fifth century B.C., is a riddle, something characteristic of his poetry. What is it we desire most? What we desire most is wisdom (*sophia*), and wisdom is a knowledge of things divine and human and the causes of each. The purpose of Athenaeus's work is to let us know what it means to be wise in a particular way. What the *Deipnosophistai* offer us are the pleasures of the pursuit of wisdom, joined with the pleasures of the table.

Chapter 4

The Cookbooks: Apicius and Artusi

> Arriving at an authentic version
> of a recipe with a long tradition
> requires work. . . . It is important
> to compare many different sources,
> printed and oral, *especially* the
> oldest available ones.
>
> Giuliano Bugialli
> *On Pasta*

The Standard of Tradition

There are two epistemologies of cookery. One is Cartesian, the other is Vichian. In his *Discourse on the Method*, Descartes puts aside history as a basis for right reasoning. He holds that nothing solid can be built upon custom and tradition. Right reasoning is based on the determination of clear and distinct ideas. The light of reason will supply the means needed to solve any problem. The right method rightly applied will yield the desired result.[1]

In his *New Science concerning the Common Nature of the Nations*, Vico advocates the axiom that doctrines should take their beginning from that of the matters which they treat. We can rightly comprehend anything in the human world by approaching it historically, that is, by grasping its particular form of development. Reason lets us make sense of the nature of things by bringing out the inner principles of their development. Tradition hands us the products of human activities as they have been realized in their natural course.

The treasure-house of tradition is there for us to take up and extend.[2]

There are two senses of eating. One is to eat in a restaurant, with dishes prepared in a commercial kitchen under the direction of a chef. The other is to eat homemade dishes prepared in a family kitchen. It is not by accident that "chef" and "restaurant" are French terms. One associates them with Auguste Escoffier (1847–1935), who established the prestige of French cooking throughout the world. He held the title of "the king of chefs and the chef of kings," and much of his career was associated with the Savoy Hotel, in London. He is the author of several authoritative culinary writings, including *La Guide Culinaire*. French cooking was not always a standard. When Caterina de Medici went to France, to marry Henri II, the future king, she took with her fifty cooks, who introduced foods and methods of cooking unknown in France, such as petits pois, artichokes, and Béchamel sauce.

In contrast to the French restaurant is the Italian tradition of the *trattoria*, in which dishes consistent with those eaten at home are prepared; the courses of the meal are cooked to order and served in a simple, unpretentious manner. The *trattoria* (like the bistro, pub, or diner) is a Vichian institution. The restaurant is a Cartesian institution, in which plates are perfected by a chef working out methods of elaborate preparation, complicated combinations, reductions, et cetera.

There is no question that Escoffier is the conventional standard for the extraordinary European meal, perhaps eaten today at a fine, expensive restaurant only on special occasions. The Cartesian mindset inhabits the practice of chefs even in more ordinary restaurants today. This mindset is responsible for the creation of "stacked food," described in Chapter 1, above. Chefs following their own sense of "right reasoning" create combinations that impress the uninformed public and those who author food columns. These chefs are trained and the food writers are informed. They take themselves very seriously. However, they demonstrate little real sense of tradition and the standard it sets. The Vichian mindset is to look to history in order to direct one's actions. History is the true teacher in all things human. This principle applies to cookery.

Giuliano Bugialli embodies this Vichian sense of cookery in all his books, including his comments introducing his collection of recipes for the preparation of pasta dishes. Pasta has become a universal culinary phenomenon, as worldwide as pizza. In so many American restaurants one encounters a list of pasta dishes with sauces combining ingredients that make no sense but which are the invention of the reasoning of the chef. Furthermore, they are most often presented as main courses, instead of a first course following an antipasto. Bugialli says that his purpose "is to provide a model of traditional Italian pasta dishes that have stood the test of centuries in Italy." He hopes that by his so doing we "can avoid the trial and error of undirected 'creativity.'" He says, rightly, that: "Innovation without such guidelines has produced some bizarre combinations that might have temporary shock value, but which don't endure for an educated palate." To cook properly, "a foundation of basic techniques, methods, and information must be established. Some combinations now being touted as new and innovative were in fact rejected ages ago in Italy."[3]

The standard of tradition is the corrective to "undirected creativity." Tradition brings about great truths and their applications that have developed from the collective expertise of a culture. No amount of new ideas, novel techniques, and experimental dishes are a substitute for the depth of tradition. Nothing can be thought of that has not already been thought. Novelty in the sense of what stands outside of tradition and does not come from the directions present in tradition is useless in general, and specifically in regard to cookery.

Recipes are the product of collective memory formulated through personal experience. A recipe, like a song, exists through repetition. A song sung only once is without significance. The point of a song or of anything musical is that it can be experienced over and over. A recipe that is employed only once is a recipe without any true significance. If the point of the recipe is simply to be novel, it is a bad recipe. A recipe is a *topos*; it is a commonplace from which a particular dish is drawn forth. Each time a recipe is used to produce a dish, that dish is a variation on a theme. The recipe is a universal become concrete as it is realized in the dish it makes possible. In the act of cooking the memory of the collective is enacted in the personal on a daily basis. Not much is required in order simply to eat, but to eat well both the recipe and the ability to enact it are required.

The science of cookery is the knowledge needed to understand the ingredients of a recipe and to bring it forth as a dish. In this sense the enactment of a recipe is like a scientific experiment. Realizing the recipe verifies its truth. Otherwise, the recipe remains an unverified hypothesis. Over time the recipe may be modified, dependent upon the availability of ingredients, alteration of tastes, and so forth. Very many of the best recipes require no more than four or five ingredients. This fact is in sharp contrast to the world of chefs, running their own restaurants, seeking to create their "signature dishes," involving a long list of tiny amounts of ingredients, often put together through complicated techniques. Over and against this world of chefs and food critics and columnists stand those who can simply cook exceptional dishes, as opposed to manipulating techniques.

In addition to practicing the science of the recipe, the cook must have the imagination connected to *bricolage*. It is the ability to combine and recombine what is available to achieve a result. It works with what is already there to obtain satisfaction. The cook must be able not only to produce excellent dishes but also to create meals, that is, to conceive of dishes that go together as courses. To eat well is not simply to eat a well prepared dish but to eat a well prepared meal. The cook must be able to enter the kitchen stocked with various foodstuffs and condiments and assemble a full meal, realizing that some of what is present can become an appetizer, something else can be the basis for a first course, other items can be combined into a main dish, and so on to dessert. The everyday meal is the product of the imagination, not of a process of systematic reason. All art is to an extent bricolage, as is the art of the meal.

The everyday meal comes and goes, but it is part of what one is, in the sense that one is what one eats and how one eats. To cook what one eats and what others with whom we dine may eat is a rudimentary form of self-knowledge. Cookery is an extension of the self into the world. In the *Phaedo*, Socrates says to Crito that to speak badly is not only damaging to language, it does some harm to the soul (*psychē*) (115e). The same may be said of cooking and eating. To produce meals that are not pleasurable and healthy is not only damaging to the art of dining, it does some harm to the soul. The harm is the failure to pursue excellence in one's affairs. It is to be lacking in *savior faire* as well as *savior vivre*. When one knows how to cook well and how to eat well, at the end of the day there is a certain satisfaction to everyday life that adds a peace to the soul. The best revenge against the adversities and unfairness encountered in ordinary existence is to cook well and eat well. The natural dialectic between cooking and dining makes possible an ongoing order to existence that aids in all other endeavors.

Apicius De Re Coquinaria

Joseph Dommers Vehling, translator of the first English edition of the cookbook of Apicius, begins his opening remarks with the assertion: "Anyone who would know something worthwhile about the private and public lives of the ancients should be well acquainted with their table. Then as now the oft quoted maxim stands that man is what he eats."[4] This view of understanding the Romans not in terms of the great events of their history and figures, but in terms of the forms of their everyday life, is in accord with Vico's claim in his oration, "On the Sumptuous Dinners of the Romans,"[5] as remarked upon in Chapter 1 herein. The Romans are all too often approached in terms of their military and political achievements and not in terms of their concrete way of life. The Roman table and the Italian table, and to an extent the table of Europe, is in many ways a continuum.

Apicius is the proverbial cognomen of several Roman gourmets. The most notable of these is Marcus Gavius Apicius (fl. 14–37 A.D.), who is said to have spent a fortune in his desire to procure rare foods. Pliny says "Apicius, the most gluttonous gorger of all spendthrifts, established the view that the flamingo's tongue has a specially fine flavor" (*Nat. Hist.*10.133). Juvenal mentions this kind of extravagance, commonly attributed to Marcus Gavius Apicius, but cautions that such attributions are not always true. "We witness many things that poor mean Apicius didn't do" (*Sat.*4.22–23). It is held by tradition that Marcus Gavius Apicius, when his fortune was somewhat reduced, took his own life, in fear that one day he would exhaust his fortune and starve to death.

Marcus Gavius Apicius is not the author of the *De Re Coquinaria*. In what is known of the book itself the text is ascribed to Caelius Apicius and it was likely compiled in its present form in the fourth century. Vehling says: "In our opinion, unfounded of course by positive proof, the Apicius book is somewhat of a gastronomic bible, consisting of ten different books by several authors, originating in Greece and taken over by the Romans along with the rest of Greek culture as spoils of war. These books, or Chapters, or fragments thereof, must have been in vogue long before they were collected and assembled in the present form."[6]

Cookbooks, even today, are more a compilation of recipes given in terms of the author's formulation than they are original creations of the author. Because of this fact, and also because of the antiquity of the Apicius book, Vehling's judgment of its origin seems plausible. No amount of puzzlement over its authorship affects in any significant manner the existence of its recipes and their importance as ancestors of today's modes of cooking.

A staple in Roman cookery, but an expensive one, was *garum* (Greek, *garos*). *Garum* was made from a small fish, *garus*, but later made from scomber or mackerel. The exact mode of preparation of *garum* is not known. There is no specific recipe for it given in Apicius's book. It is likely presupposed as an ingredient or sauce for meat dishes, and the term may have become a generic term for sauces. Vehling claims that "The original *garum* was no doubt akin to our modern anchovy sauce, at least the best quality of the ancient sauce. The principles of manufacture surely are alike. *Garum*, like our anchovy sauce, is the *purée* of a small fish, named *garus*, as yet unidentified. The fish, intestines and all, was spiced, pounded, fermented, salted, strained, and bottled for future use. The finest *garum* was made of the livers of the fish only, exposed to the sun, fermented, somehow preserved."[7]

La Cucina, the comprehensive collection of recipes of every region of Italy, produced by the Accademia Italiana della Cucina, contains a recipe from Sicily for "salsetta di mandorle e acciughe" (almond and anchovy sauce), to be used on meats and fish.[8] Toasted almonds are pounded and mixed with minced, salted fillets of anchovy and seasoned with chopped mint leaves, cinnamon, vinegar, lemon juice, and olive oil to make a creamy sauce. This sauce may be somewhat similar to the ancient *garum*, at least in principle, in that it combines pureed oily fish with spices and the acetic acid of vinegar and the citric acid of lemon. *Garum* also may be comparable to Worchestershire sauce, in the sense that this bottled sauce contains anchovies combined with garlic, cloves, and an assortment of other seasonings. Seen in this way, *garum* is not such an oddity of the Roman kitchen. Since it was also known to the Greeks, some form of spicy fish sauce may be considered a constant of ancient and modern cooking.

The most notorious dish of the Romans is dormice. In the *Cena Trimalchionis* of Petronius's *Satyricon*, the guests are presented with dormice as part of the beginning of the meal: "There were also dormice rolled in honey and poppy-seed, and supported on little bridges soldered to the plate. Then there were hot sausages laid on a silver grill, and under the grill damsons and seeds of pomegranate" (31).

According to the translator's note these were the grey, edible dormouse—*glis vulgaris*. Apicius provides a recipe for stuffed dormice (*glires*). In this recipe, the dormouse is stuffed with forcemeat of pork and small pieces of dormouse meat, pounded together with condiments and either roasted in the oven or boiled in a stockpot. Vehling claims that dormouse or *glis* "has nothing to do with mice. The fat dormouse of the South of Europe is the size of a rat, an arboreal rodent, living in trees. . . . Dormouse, as an article of diet, should not astonish Americans who relish squirrel, opossum, muskrat, 'coon,' etc."[9]

Some support for Vehling's claim is that the recipe for dormice is part of Apicius's Book 8, which contains recipes for main meat dishes of wild boar, venison, gazelle, wild sheep, beef and veal, kid and lamb, pig, and hare. I believe the right conclusion to draw is that the Romans ate two kinds of dormice, one as an appetizer and the other as a main course. The two most famous foodstuffs of the Roman table are *garum* and dormice.

Apicius's *De Re Coquinaria* is divided into ten books containing a total of 467 recipes. Its first recipe is for spiced wine made with honey, a kind of mead with which Roman meals usually began. Book 1 generally concerns the preparation and preservation of various ingredients. These instructions are of special importance when one considers that refrigeration, and the means taken for granted in the modern kitchen to preserve food, were not there for the ancient cook. Book 2 concerns minced dishes of meat or fish, and sausages. They suggest dishes that might be used as appetizers. Book 3 contains instructions for the preparation of a wide range of vegetables, including asparagus, squash, cucumbers, cauliflower, leeks, beets, turnips, celery, cabbage, endive, lettuce, cardoons, carrots, and parsnips. To keep vegetables green, Apicius recommends boiling with baking soda (not often recommended today). He also includes instructions for a complete vegetable dinner, easily digested.

Book 4 contains a number of miscellaneous dishes of vegetables and small amounts of meat. These appear almost to be dishes for an in-between course, what in a formal Italian dinner is a *piatto di mezzo*. Book 5 concerns legumes, such as lentils, peas, beans, green beans, and chickpeas. Book 6 has recipes for various types of fowl—ostrich, crane, duck, partridge, dove, pigeon, peacock, pheasant, goose, and chicken. Book 7 is a list of sumptuous dishes. These are such dishes as pork cutlets, fresh ham, pig paunch, liver and lungs, salt pork, mushrooms, cheese and honey, snails, and eggs (fried, boiled, or poached).

Book 8, as described above, contains main meat courses, including dormouse, the last recipe in the list. Book 9 is a counterpart to Book 8, presenting an array of seafood—shellfish, ray, calamari, octopus, oysters, sea urchins, mussels, sardines, et cetera. Book 10 concentrates on a number of fish sauces, complementing the subject of Book 9. Vehling comments: "The absence of books on bread and cake baking, dessert cookery, indicates that the present Apicius is not complete."[10]

Apicius's book is ordered in much the same way as modern cookbooks, or perhaps it is more correct to say that they follow its original order. It begins with a discussion of ingredients and basic techniques, proceeds to what might be served as appetizers, then to vegetable preparations and main meat dishes, as well as some special dishes. A major variation between modern cookbooks and Apicius's are the last two books on fish. Fish would normally come before meat dishes in a modern meal, at least in a meal served in the French manner. The missing book on desserts would compare to the final topic of modern cookbooks. Generally speaking, fish as food mentioned in ancient literature seems to have less status than meat.

One of the reactions to Roman recipes, and to many of those in Apicius's book, is that some of the ingredients and their combinations are unappetizing and even seem grotesque. Indeed, it is clear that the ancients generally considered any creature to be edible in all of its parts. A counter to this modern view is given by Vehling. He gives the following "in the Apician style or writing: Take liquamen [any kind of culinary liquid], pepper, cayenne, eggs, lemon, olive oil, vinegar, white wine, anchovies, onions, tarragon, pickled cucumbers, parsley, chervil, hard-boiled eggs, capers, green peppers, mustard, chop, mix well, and serve."[11] Put in this way, without giving the proper sequence or amount of ingredients, this recipe seems to be just a strange concoction. It is, however, according to Vehling, the recipe for tartar sauce. The inclusion of anchovies and hard-boiled eggs, as well as green peppers, makes it rather an elaborate version of tartar sauce—which today would more likely be mayonnaise, onions, and capers or pickle relish. But his point is well taken.

If we carefully read *De Re Coquinaria* we see similarities with what we eat today. What we do not see is the structure of the full Roman feast that required a large number of slaves, each with a particular duty:

dispensator . . . . organized the other slaves; apportioned work
ostiarius . . . . porter who oversaw all who entered and exited
atriensis . . . . supervised the atrium; guarded arms, trophies, etc.
obsonator . . . . purchased meat, fruit, and delicacies from the market
vocatores . . . . delivered invitations; received and placed the guests
cubicularii . . . . arranged the tables and couches
dapiferi . . . . brought the dishes into the dining room
nomenculatores . . . . . informed the guests of the qualities of each dish
structor . . . . arranged the dishes symmetrically
praegustator . . . . chief taster who sampled every dish
triclinarche . . . . chief steward who oversaw the progress of the meal
procillatores . . . . young slaves who attended to each guest's needs
sandaligeruli . . . . removed and replaced the guests' sandals
adversitores . . . . conducted the guests home by torchlight

In addition to the cooks and kitchen staff, there were slaves who entertained the guests and many more menial slaves: *flabellarii*, who cooled the guests with peacocks' feathers; *focarii*, who attended to the fires; *scoparii*, who swept the apartments; and *peniculi*, who cleaned the banqueting tables.[12]

For the patrician Roman host of a banquet labor was not an issue, but desired ingredients were difficult to secure, and expensive. For the modern large dinner or banquet the labor of its preparation can be expensive, but good ingredients are affordable and readily available.

La scienza in cucina e l'arte di mangiar bene

"In 1910, upon reaching its fourteenth edition (the last to be printed under the author's supervision), Pellegrino Artusi's *La scienza in cucina e l'arte di mangiar bene* began to be recognized as the most significant Italian cookbook of modern times."[13] Pellegrino Artusi died on March 30 of that year. The first edition of his cookbook had appeared in 1891. The appearance of the fourteenth edition brought the total number of copies sold to 52,000. It is difficult to imagine that the library of any Italian kitchen would lack a copy of Artusi's book. *La Cucina*, of the Accademia Italiana della Cucina, mentioned above, that covers the cooking of all the regions of Italy, contains 2,000 recipes. Artusi's book of 790 recipes is the work of a single author.

Pellegrino Artusi was born in 1820, the son of a prominent textile merchant, in Forlimpopoli in Emilia-Romagna. As an investment banker and investor in railroad stocks and treasury bonds, Artusi made a fortune in a little more than ten years and was thus able to withdraw from active business. He took up residence in Florence, where he dedicated himself to his intellectual and culinary interests. He composed his masterpiece, *La scienza in cucina*, as a personal diversion. Advised by friends that it had no future, he published it at his own expense and dedicated it to his two white cats, Biancani and Sibillone. He conducted the sales and distribution himself. The book became a bestseller in its subsequent editions, which expanded its number of recipes from 475 to 790, as in the fourteenth edition.

Eating well, for Artusi as for most writers of cookbooks, is not simply an art of producing pleasure; it is also an art promoting health. His title page carries the motto "Igiene, Economia, Buon Gusto" (Health, Economics, Good Taste).[14] Economics here is home economics, just as Aristotle understood it in his treatise on *Economics*, in which he says: "It is clear, therefore, that it must be the function of economic science both to found a household and to make use of it" (1343a). The subtitle of Artusi's work is "Manuale pratico per le famiglie" (Practical manual for families). The family and the household it entails are the foundation of society. The center of the family is the hearth and home cooking.

Artusi's title page emphasizes the connection of the art of eating well with four epigraphical statements. The first is: "Un pasto buono ed un mezzano mantengon l'uomo sano [A good meal and so a means to maintain a healthy human being]." The second is: "Molto cibo e mal digesto non fa il corpo sano e lesto [Much food and bad digestion does not make a healthy and agile body]." Artusi advises to acquire the habit of eating everything, but not to become a slave to one's stomach. A third statement in his title page is: "Piglia il cibo con misura dai due regni di natura [Take food with measure from the two kingdoms of nature]" that is, from "il regno vegetale [the vegetable kingdom]" and "il regno animale [the animal kingdom]." A meal should be balanced. In a forth epigraph Artusi gives in Latin the Italian proverb "La prima digestione si fa in bocca," that is, "*Prima digestio fit in ore* [Digestion is first done in the mouth]."

In his remarks on "Alcune norme d'igiene [Some norms of health]," Artusi advises diners to chew food well. He also says that the solution for disturbed digestion may often be to abstain from eating for a period. He uses his cat Sibillone as a guide. He says that "my very dear friend Sibillone, when experiencing indigestion, would refrain from eating for a day or two."[15] He says that often animals, with the natural instincts, teach us how to behave. The cats are not simply a clever dedication of the book; they play a role in Artusi's thinking. He also insists that good health requires adequate exercise. His cats run over the rooftops; he takes daily walks. Artusi also warns against drinking too much wine and the abuse of liquors.

As part of his discussion of health Artusi treats of when the meals of the day should be taken. He advocates a very light breakfast or none at all, depending upon how one feels from the meals of the previous day. He recommends black coffee and a half glass of water. If one desires more, he recommends black coffee with a piece of buttered toast, or coffee with some milk in it, or a cup of hot chocolate. This is much in accord with the standard Florentine *prima colazione* of *caffellatte* (coffee and warm milk) with bread, butter, and jam or *marmellata*.

He then speaks of the "modern" custom of "lunch," *seconda colazione* or *colazione solida*, taken at eleven or noon. He advises not to overeat, as the main meal will follow in the evening, and he advises to separate this luncheon meal from the evening dinner by seven hours. Artusi refers to this midday meal as *pranzo*. But *pranzo* connotes a full-course meal. *Pranzare* is to dine. Artusi then speaks of "la beata usanza de nostri padri di pranzare a mezzogiorno [the blessed custom of our fathers to dine at midday]."[16]

Having lived in Florence, I am astonished that Artusi places the principal meal of the day in the evening instead of midday (midday being understood in this context as one o'clock, or slightly later). By tradition, the shops and offices in Florence close at one o'clock for all to return home for the main meal of the day. Shops reopen and work resumes in the later afternoon. The evening meal or *cena* is a light repast, taken before retiring for the night. In Southern Italy the main meal of the day is taken even later than midday—more in accord with the practice of the ancient Romans. Because the schedule of the modern business day is becoming more and more prevalent, the main meal of the day, for many, now is being pushed to the evening. For Artusi to advocate this schedule, well more than a century ago, is inexplicable.

Antonio Carluccio, in remarks on "The Italian Meal," that begin his cookbook of 1986, says: "There is no doubt Italians live for food. They think and talk about it constantly and they spend a lot of money on it. The high point of the day is the midday meal." Of the other two meals, he says: "For most Italians in the towns and cities breakfast is just an espresso. Anyone who is hungry will have a panino (a bread roll with a savoury filling) at a café. Or they will eat brioche or little cakes. . . . The evening meal, like breakfast, is a fairly minor event. It is usually quite light, perhaps a little brodino or an omelette, and it is often eaten quite late." Carluccio points out that in Italian towns and cities all activity stops in order to have the midday meal, and says the midday meal: "demonstrates the true artistry of Italian cooking. It is planned so that each course is in harmony with all the others: the tastes, the textures, the richness and the quantities are all perfectly balanced."[17] Every Italian has been brought up to know food and to know exactly how any dish should taste.

A further anomaly in Artusi's account is his claim that the Florentines have the custom of having the appetizer course after the first course of soup, risotto, or pasta. He says: "Appetizers [principii] or antipasti are, properly speaking, those delicious trifles that are made to be eaten either after the pasta course, as is practiced in Tuscany, which seems preferable to me, or before, as is done elsewhere in Italy."[18] This is not true today in Tuscany. Antipasti, as the term states, appear before the *pasto*, the courses that make up the meal. According to Artusi's statement, his personal preference is that the little dishes of antipasti or *principii* are an interlude between the first course and the second.

The only justification I can conceive for this practice is that, when one comes to the table very hungry, the hunger is immediately satisfied by the dish of pasta. It is true that once one begins to eat the pasta one does not stop until it is consumed, and then the diners relax. The home-cooked Tuscan meal does not always begin with antipasti; it can begin directly with the pasta course. Antipasti are simply skipped. In the menus that Artusi includes at the end of his book, that are arranged by the months of the year, not all menus include antipasti or *principii*, but those that do have them following the first course. The antipasti recipe section of Artusi's book is quite short. All but one of these are recipes for *crostini* (canapés), including the one most preferred in Florence—*crostini di fegatini di pollo* (canapés with chicken livers). The exception is a purée of *baccalà* (salted codfish) mixed with cream. It, too, Artusi says, can be served with the addition of *crostini*.[19]

Luigi Ballerini says: "It is doubtful that Artusi ever touched a kitchen utensil, that he ever lit a fire under a pot or finely chopped or gently stirred anything,"[20] These tasks, Ballerini claims, were done by Artusi's housekeeper and cook, Francesco Ruffilli and Marietta Sabbatini, Artusi's faithful retainers. Very likely Artusi did little routine kitchen work, but that he is so precise and passionate about his recipes, and his narratives, witticisms, and comments that accompany them, suggests he had direct experience in the preparation of dishes. He was more than just a taster and critic of what his two retainers did. No one truly attached to the science of cookery does not actually cook. Apicius certainly had slave labor in running his kitchen, but he himself was truly a cook, enacting his own recipes. The need for assistance in today's kitchen is, to an extent, replaced by modern stoves, ovens, and appliances such as food processors and blenders.

Artusi's recipes, like those of Apicius and most modern cookbooks, embrace the range of the preparation of sauces, eggs, fried foods, boiled and roasted meats, vegetables and legumes, types of fish, cold dishes, and desserts (see the comment above on the lack of desserts in Apicius's book). Artusi endorses ending a meal with ice cream (*gelato*), especially in summer. He believes desserts of ice cream aid digestion. He says: "And today, thanks to the American ice cream makers, which have triple action and need no spatula, making ice cream has become so much easier and faster that it would be a shame not to enjoy much more frequently the sensual pleasure of this delicious food."[21] He also ends a meal with a cup of coffee, as do Florentines today.

Although many Florentines often enjoy a *gelato*, perhaps while strolling in the evening or afternoon, everyday meals today customarily end with fresh fruit or with cheese and fruit. This final course of fruit is reflected in a number of the menus at the end of Artusi's book. He remarks that what fruit is to be included is best determined by the season.[22] The dinner menus Artusi suggests comprise two for each month of the year and ten additional ones for the holidays. Unlike present-day meals of antipasti, pasta, meat or fish and vegetable, and fruit or dessert, these menus all have seven courses, and in some cases eight, making them perhaps typical of nineteenth-century dining, although we might presume that the portions were not as large as those usually eaten today. What we find in Artusi's book are all the recipes for dishes found in Florentine dining today.

Today's Recipes, Final Remarks

Today, except as a matter of curiosity, perhaps to show it can be done, no one cooks from the books of Apicius and Artusi. They remain the grand ancestors. Some years ago we began to hear of something called the "Mediterranean diet." It was realized that, seen from a general perspective, there is a common way of eating that stretches across the top arc of the Mediterranean, from Spain and southern France to Greece, in the middle of which is the Italian peninsula. This diet is based on a healthy cookery that combines olive oil, grains, vegetables, meats, seafood, natural cheeses, nuts, fruits, and wine. The dishes made from these ingredients are eaten in moderate portions. Their preparation is simple and straightforward.

The Mediterranean diet is centered on one, full, multi-course meal, eaten daily. Such a meal can often be prepared in about an hour, from fresh ingredients. An important principle of the meal is that meat or seafood is only one of many ingredients and not the main ingredient around which the meal is formed. A proper portion of meat or seafood is about four ounces per person. A second important principle is that the meal is seldom concluded with a large, sweet dessert. It is normally ended with fresh fruit (as advocated by Artusi in his appendix of monthly menus, noted above). Prepared desserts are not excluded but are not served every day. The details of this meal have been discussed in Chapter 1. The Mediterranean diet has largely come and gone in the popular consciousness, as is true of all such diets. But it persists in its countries of origin, as it has for centuries. It is simply the natural way of cooking and eating among these populations. It is the way of cooking and eating that I personally advocate and practice.

All cooks must settle on several cookbooks to which they return regularly, to prompt and guide what may make up the day's main meal. I turn to three authors and the primary cookbook of each, although I also consult other of their works. The primary books are: Giuliano Bugialli, *The Fine Art of Italian Cooking*;[23] Marcella Hazan, *Essentials of Classic Italian Cooking*;[24] and Michele Scicolone, *The Antipasto Table*.[25] Bugialli's recipes, as noted in Chapter 1, are Florentine, although his other books span all the regions of Italy.[26] Some of Hazan's recipes reflect her residence in Venice, but her work goes generally through Italian dishes.[27] Scicolone is an Italian-American with close connections to Italy; her works have many recipes derived from southern Italian cuisine.[28] Her book of antipasti is unique—a treasure-house of such dishes. There is almost no antipasto that cannot be found therein.

In addition to these three books there is a "fourth," that consists of those specific recipes I find of interest from various other books that have accumulated in my library. Although all cookbooks contain a great number of recipes, often one finds only one or two of special interest, and to find these makes the book valuable. In addition to such individualized books there are works to consult that are quite specialized, for example: *Il libro d'oro dei primi piatti italiani*, containing 1,000 recipes of first courses only.[29]

Marcella Hazan says of Italian cooking: "It is not the created, not to speak of 'creative,' cooking of restaurant chefs. It is the cooking that spans remembered history that has evolved during the whole course of transmitted skills and intuitions in homes throughout the Italian peninsula and the islands, in its hamlets, on its farms, in its great cities. It is cooking from the home kitchen." Hazan's point concerning "creative" cooking as opposed to that which has been inherited from tradition is in agreement with that quoted from Bugialli in Chapter 1 and in the epigraph to this chapter. No one who understands the nature of home cooking can believe that the creations of restaurant chefs can in any sense become a replacement for it.

Hazan continues: "Of course there have been—and there still are—aristocrats' homes, merchants' homes, peasants' homes, but however disparate the amenities, they have one vital thing in common: Food, whether simple or elaborate, is cooked in the style of the family. There is no such thing as Italian *haute cuisine* because there are no high or low roads in Italian cooking. All roads lead to the home, to *la cucina di casa*—the only one that deserves to be called Italian cooking."[30] Thus cooking presupposes the reality of home and the sense of the family. Cooking of meals, home, and family are a dialectic at the basis of human life, lived naturally and pleasurably. They provide us with an image of peace in which our everyday affairs can proceed *con calma*.

I would add a word here regarding a little book by Hazan, *Ingredienti*, left partially finished at her death and completed by her husband, Victor.[31] It is unique, a modern classic in which, on the basis of a lifetime of experience with home cooking, Hazan sets down her thoughts on how to understand and use the most basic ingredients of the Italian table. Anyone, no matter how good a cook, can benefit from it. The science of cookery begins with a knowledge of ingredients—how to assess their freshness and how to preserve them. Without such knowledge, no dish can be properly prepared One eats what one grows or buys. To select the right ingredients requires the good eye, the *buon occhio*.

The Florentine historian Francesco Guicciardini says: "All that which has been in the past and is at present will be again in the future. Both the names and the appearances change, so that he who does not have a good eye will not recognize them. Nor will he know how to grasp a norm of conduct or make a judgment by means of observation."[32] What is true of the art of prudence in human conduct in general is true of the human art of dining. The good eye is the ability to grasp the truth present in tradition and to incorporate it into one's everyday actions. The meal is a microcosm of human sociability. Repetition, not novelty, is the key to the art of dining.

I anticipate that, if the reader has been able to give attention to the pages of this text so far, that reader has raised the question of what is to be said of other traditions of cooking and dining. I have said little of French food, or of that of northern Europe generally. Clearly one can eat well throughout Europe and, with discretion, one can eat well anywhere. So much has been written on French cuisine that it seems unnecessary to say more, even if I felt in the position to do so. I leave French cooking to Julia Child, *Mastering the Art of French Cooking*,[33] and to Escoffier, Brillat-Savarin, and the *Larousse Gastronomique*.

Much of what I have said of home cooking, I believe, could be said of the great virtues of Indian, Chinese,

Japanese, Thai, and Asian cooking generally[34] and of Persian and Middle Eastern cooking.[35] These are whole cuisines with their own great principles and tastes. Unique to American cooking is that of the South, with its well-known emphasis on cooked greens, fried chicken and catfish, varieties of barbeque, and desserts such as sweet-potato pie.[36] There are specialties of the Mexican table, in particular those of the "corn kitchen,"[37] and of the countries of South America, e.g., the *churrasco* of Brazil and the *chimichurri* sauce of Argentina that accompanies grilled meats. There are also the dishes distinctive to the many cultures of the continent of Africa, such as West African yam stuffing for chicken. It is not possible to characterize adequately all the aspects of the world's cuisine. Every culture and country has its manner of food preparation and dining, and their dishes should be enjoyed whenever possible, without question.[38] In advancing my views I have kept to what I know and to the meals of my own home cooking, done on a daily basis.

Restaurant "stacked" food, as remarked on in Chapter 1, has its predecessor in the doctrine of *nouvelle-cuisine*, that reduced the preparation of food and dining to presentation, in which tidbits of food were placed on plates with dots of colorful sauces, in imitation of abstract expressionist painting. Stacked food is more hearty. The diner is faced with a kind of *Eintopfgericht* (a one-pot meal) assembled on a plate. There can be no doubt but that restaurant dining will take on a new form. What its successor will be remains to be seen, but we can be certain it will be governed by a theory of presentation, not of cooking. None of this fascination with presentation by chefs and their food critics is necessary or even interesting. As the best food is simple, prepared with few and fresh ingredients, the home-cooked meal needs no garnish. The food to be eaten should look like itself.

To eat well we depend upon the five senses, the first of which, in this regard, is taste. Taste is acquired from childhood but is cultivated in adulthood. Necessary to taste are smell and sight. The home-cooked meal is first present in the smells coming from the kitchen, a sensation that no restaurant can produce properly. Food must also be seen. Diners sit in anticipation as the dishes are brought to the table. Touch is present in terms of the consistency of what is eaten. Vegetables should not be over- or undercooked. Bread should be firm but moist. Pasta should not be overcooked, *stracotta*, lest it become a *porcheria* (an indecency). Meat must be tender. Cheese must be brought to room temperature. Fruit must be firm or soft, depending on what kind it is. Sound has its role in the kitchen, to verify whether oil is sufficiently hot for something to be properly fried or something is simmering too hard or too little. Sound fully enters the meal in the form of conversation. Overall, cooking and dining are among the activities that make us know we have five senses and we are a linguistic and embodied animal.

In his *First and Second Discourses*, Rousseau connects manners and morals, the two principal meanings of the French word *moeurs*.[39] Civilized human conduct is governed by manners. The morality of everyday life is a matter of manners. Manners are learned from childhood, and once learned they are a guide for life. They are, in fact, the logic of civilized life—of personal self-control and grace. A great and indispensable source for the acquisition of manners is the table manners communicated to children by their parents and relatives. To have manners, like the ability to read and speak well, once acquired, is a good for life.

Table manners require the meal. When the meal disappears, manners disappear with it. To spend one's days eating fast food, beginning with a breakfast sandwich, eaten with the hands, and ending the day with a commercially prepared food, heated for a minute in a microwave oven, requires no sense of table manners. An upbringing of eating on this pattern leaves the contemporary person at a loss for any sense of manners in general.

The home-cooked meal disappears, even as a childhood memory. There is a morality to the home-cooked meal that resides in table manners, a sense of things and of conversation about them. Fast-food feeding during the days of the week, and dining out on weekends, do not accomplish the sense of things, the self-knowledge of the home-cooked meal and of the meal extended to the pleasure of dining at home, with friends.

What are we to conclude? With the question of table manners we are brought back to the Socratic assertion in the *Phaedo* (115e), that to speak badly is not only faulty so far as the language goes but it does some harm to the soul. Speaking and eating are at the basis of the human condition. To engage in either or both badly does some harm to the human soul.

Notes

Chapter 1. Introduction

1. Interlinear citations to Greek and Latin works are to the Loeb Classical Library editions of Harvard University Press, except for quotations from the Platonic dialogues, which are from Plato, *Complete Works*, ed. John M. Cooper (Indianapolis: Hackett, 1997), and from Aristotle's treatises, found in *The Complete Works of Aristotle*, ed. Jonathan Barnes, 2 vols. (Princeton: Princeton University Press, 1984).

2. Giambattista Vico, *The New Science of Giambattista Vico*, trans. Thomas Goddard Bergin and Max Harold Fisch (Ithaca: Cornell University Press, 1984), par. 539.

3. Mircea Eliade, *The Forge and the Crucible*, trans. Stephen Corrin (New York: Harper, 1962), 79.

4. Ibid., 78.

5. Vico, *New Science*, par. 801.

6. Ibid.

7. Ibid.

8. Ibid.

9. See Athenaeus, *The Learned Banqueters*, trans. S. Douglas Olson, 7 vols. (Cambridge: Harvard University Press, 2006).

10. Juan Luis Vives, "A Fable About Man," trans. Nancy Lenkeith, in *The Renaissance Philosophy of Man*, ed. Ernst Cassirer, Paul Oskar Kristeller, and John Herman Randall, Jr. (Chicago: University of Chicago Press, 1948), 387–93.

11. Giambattista Vico, "On the Sumptuous Dinners of the Romans," trans. George A. Trone, *New Vico Studies* 20 (2002): 79–89. See also the commentary, Donald Phillip Verene, "Vico and Culinary Art: 'On the Sumptuous Dinners of the Romans' and the Science of the First Meals," *New Vico Studies* 20 (2002): 69–78.

12. Regarding Roman dining generally, see Jérôme Carcopino, *Daily Life in Ancient Rome*, trans. E. O. Lorimer (New Haven: Yale University Press, 1940). See also, Ilaria Gozzini Giacosa, *A Taste of Ancient Rome*, trans. Anna Herklotz (Chicago: University of Chicago Press, 1992); Patrick Faas, *Around the Roman Table*. trans. Shaun Whiteside (Chicago: University of Chicago Press, 1994); and Ugo Enrico Paoli, *Vita romana* (Florence: Le Monnier, 1958).

13. *Apicius: Cookery and Dining in Imperial Rome*, trans. Joseph Dommers Vehling (New York: Dover, 1977), 22.

14. Pellegrino Artusi, *La scienza in cucina e l'arte di mangiar bene* (Florence: Marzocco, 1960).

15. Ibid., 119. My translation.

16. Giuliano Bugialli, *The Fine Art of Italian Cooking* (New York: Quadrangle, 1977), 3.

17. Ibid., 6.

18. Ibid., 7. My translation. See also, Gillian Riley, *Renaissance Recipes* (San Francisco: Pomegranate Artbooks, 1993).

19. On the history of pasta see Gillian Riley, *The Oxford Companion to Italian Food* (New York: Oxford University Press, 2007), 372–74.

20. Odile Redon, Françoise Sabban, and Silvano Serrenti, *The Medieval Kitchen: Recipes from France and Italy*, trans. Edward Schneider (Chicago: University of Chicago Press, 1998), 13.

21. *Bugialli on Pasta* (New York: Simon and Schuster, 1988), 9.

22. Pastern is the term for a part of the foot of an equine that lies between the fetlock and the coffin joint.

23. Vehling, "The Book of Apicius," in *Apicius*, 27–28.

24. Jean-Anthelme Brillat-Savarin, *The Physiology of Taste*, trans. Anne Drayton (New York: Penguin, 1994), 13–14. An earlier edition of this same translation was published by Penguin, with the title rendered as *The Philosopher in the Kitchen* (1970). In regard to the theme of the

philosopher in the kitchen, see the recipes and their presentation in the cookbook: Francine Segan, *The Philosopher's Kitchen* (New York: Random House, 2004).

25. Brillat-Savarin, *Physiology*, 176.
26. Ibid., 161.
27. Ibid., 132.
28. Ibid., 36.
29. Ibid., 132.
30. Ibid., 162.
31. Ibid., 165.
32. Ibid., 166.

Chapter 2. The Dinner of the Seven Wise Men

1. Plutarch, "The Dinner of the Seven Wise Men," in vol. 2 of *Moralia*, trans. Frank Cole Babbitt (Cambridge: Harvard University Press, 2002), 346–449.
2. See *Early Greek Philosophy*, vol. 2, *Beginnings and Early Ionian Thinkers*, Part 1, ed. and trans. André Laks and Glenn W. Most (Cambridge: Harvard University Press, 2016), 245.
3. Ibid.
4. Ibid., 227.
5. Ibid., 265.
6. Giambattista Vico, *New Science*, par. 416.
7. Giovanni Pico della Mirandola, "Oration on the Dignity of Man," trans. Elizabeth Livermore Forbes, in *The Renaissance Philosophy of Man*, ed. E. Cassirer, Paul Oscar Kristeller, and John Herman Randall, Jr. (Chicago: University of Chicago Press, 1948), 235.

Chapter 3. The Learned Banqueters

1. E.g., Eva Zane, *Greek Cooking for the Gods* (San Francisco: 101 Productions, 1974), 8, 22, 84, 144, 166, 186. Quotations from Athenaeus are used as epigraphs for sections of recipes for various courses.
2. Prosper Montagné, *Larousse Gastronomique*, trans. Nina Froud et al. (New York: Crown, 1961), 67.

3. S. Douglas Olson, "Introduction," vol. 1 of the *Learned Banqueters* (Cambridge: Harvard University Press, 2006), ix–x.

4. Ibid., x.

5. Giuliano Bugialli, *The Fine Art of Italian Cooking* (New York: Quadrangle, 1977), 7.

6. See *Early Greek Philosophy*, vol. 5, *Western Greek Thinkers*, Part 2, ed. and trans. André Laks and Glenn W. Most (Cambridge: Harvard University Press, 2016), 371.

7. See H. B. Gottschalk, *Heraclides of Pontus* (Oxford: Clarendon, 1980), chap. 2.

Chapter 4. The Cookbooks: Apicius and Artusi

1. René Descartes, *Discourse on the Method of Rightly Conducting One's Reason and Seeking Truth in the Sciences*, in vol. 1 of *The Philosophical Writings of Descartes*, trans. J. Cottingham, R. Stoothoff, and D. Murdoch (Cambridge: Cambridge University Press, 1985), pt. 2.

2. Giambattista Vico, *The New Science of Giambattista Vico*, trans. Thomas Goddard Bergin and Max Harold Fisch (Ithaca, NY: Cornell University Press, 1984), axiom 106, par. 314.

3. *Bugialli on Pasta* (New York: Simon and Schuster, 1988), 8.

4. Joseph Dommers Vehling, "The Book of Apicius," in *Apicius, Cookery and Dining in Imperial Rome* (New York: Dover, 1977), 3.

5. Giambattista Vico, "On the Sumptuous Dinners of the Romans," trans. George A. Trone, *New Vico Studies* 20 (2002): 79–89.

6. Vehling, "Apicius," 12.

7. Ibid., 22.

8. Accademia Italiana della Cucina, *La Cucina: The Regional Cooking of Italy* [Italian title: *La Cucina del Bel Paese*], trans. Jay Hyams (New York: Rizzoli, 2009), 75.

9. *Apicius*, 205.
10. Vehling, "Apicius," 43.
11. Ibid., 27.
12. *Schott's Food and Drink Miscellany* (New York: Bloomsbury, 2004), 35.
13. Luigi Ballerini, "Introduction," in Pellegrino Artusi, *Science in the Kitchen and the Art of Eating Well*, trans. Murtha Baca and Stephen Sartarelli (Toronto: University of Toronto Press, 2003), xv.
14. Pellegrino Artusi, *La Scienza in cucina e l'arte di mangiar bene* (Florence: Marzocco, 1980).
15. Ibid., 23.
16. Ibid., 22.
17. Antonio Carluccio, "The Italian Meal," in *A Taste of Italy* (Boston: Little Brown, 1986), 8–11.
18. Artusi, *Science*, 110; *Scienza*, 110.
19. Ibid., 110–16; 110–16.
20. Ballerini, "Introduction," xlix.
21. Artusi, *Science*, 545; *Scienza*, 499.
22. Ibid., 584; 534.
23. Giuliano Bugialli, *The Fine Art of Italian Cooking: The Classic Cookbook, Updated and Expanded* (New York: Gramercy, 2005; orig. pub. 1977).
24. Marcella Hazan, *Essentials of Classic Italian Cooking* (New York: Knopf, 1993).
25. Michele Scicolone, *The Antipasto Table* (New York: William Morrow, 1991).
26. E.g., in addition to *Bugialli on Pasta*, rev. ed. (New York: Stewart, Tabori and Chang, 2000), see his *Foods of Tuscany* (New York: Stewart, Tabori and Chang, 1992) and *Foods of Italy* (New York: Stewart, Tabori and Chang, 1984).
27. E.g., *Marcella Cucina* (New York: Harper Collins, 1977), *Marcella's Italian Kitchen* (New York: Knopf, 1986), and *Marcella Says . . .* (New York: Harper Collins, 2004). Regarding Venetian cooking, see Damiano Martin, *The da Fiori Cookbook* (New York: William Morrow, 2003).

28. E.g., *A Fresh Taste of Italy* (New York: Broadway Books, 1997) and *1,000 Italian Recipes* (New York: Wiley, 2004).

29. Fiamma Niccolini Adimari and Fosco Provvedi, *Il libro d'oro dei primi piatti italiani con 1000 ricette* (Milan: Mursia, 1980). Paolo Petroni, *Il libro della vera cucina fiorentina* (Florence: Bonechi, 1974) and Lynne Rossetto Kasper, *The Splendid Table: Recipes from Emilia-Romagna* (New York: William Morrow, 1992) are examples of books with very specific emphasis. The largest compendium of recipes of Italian cooking is the 1263-page *The Silver Spoon* (New York: Phaidon, 2005), originally conceived and published in 1950 by *Domus*, the Italian design and architectural magazine, with the title *Il cucchiaio d'argento*. Nearly as large, and quite authoritative, is *La Cucina*, compiled by the Italian Academy of Cuisine (see note 8, above).

30. Hazan, *Essentials*, 5.

31. Marcella Hazan and Victor Hazan, *Ingredienti* (New York: Scribner, 2016).

32. Francesco Guicciardini, *Ricordi* (Milan: Rizzoli, 1977), 131. My translation.

33. Julia Child, *Mastering the Art of French Cooking*, vols. 1 and 2 (New York: Knopf, 1961 and 1970).

34. E.g., *Joyce Chen Cookbook* (Philadelphia: Lippincott, 1962), and Piero Antolini and The Lian Tjo, *The Great Book of Chinese Cooking* (New York: International Culinary Society, 1990).

35. E.g., Najmieh Khalili Batmanglij, *New Food of Life: Ancient Persian and Modern Iranian Cooking and Ceremonies* (Washington, D.C.: Mage Publishers, 2000).

36. For recipes see: Nathalie Dupree, *New Southern Cooking* (New York: Knopf, 1991); Edna Lewis and Scott Peacock, *The Gift of Southern Cooking* (New York: Knopf, 2003); Dora Charles, *A Real Southern Cook in Her Savannah Kitchen* (New York: Houghton Mifflin Harcourt, 2015). Regarding New Orleans cooking, I would recommend Rima Collin and Richard Collin, *The New Orleans*

Cookbook (New York: Knopf, 1997), *Chef Paul Prudhomme's Louisiana Kitchen* (New York: William Morrow, 1964), and *The Justin Wilson Gourmet and Gourmand Cookbook* (Gretna, LA: Pelican, 1989).

37. E.g., Aída Gabilondo, *Mexican Family Cooking* (New York: Fawcett Columbine, 1986).

38. For a single work that takes the reader and cook through a great range of recipes from many cultures, see *The Horizon Cookbook and Illustrated History of Eating and Drinking through the Ages*, ed. Wendy Buehr, 2 vols. (New York: American Heritage and Doubleday, 1968). The best guide to food and cooking terminology throughout the world is: Sharon Tyler Herbst, *Food Lover's Companion: Comprehensive Definitions of Nearly 6000 Food, Drink, and Culinary Terms*, 3d ed. (Hauppange, NY: Barron's, 2001).

39. Jean-Jacques Rousseau, *The First and Second Discourses*, trans. Roger D. Masters and Judith Masters (New York: St. Martin's, 1964). See also Leon R. Kass, *The Hungry Soul: Eating and the Perfecting of Our Nature* (Chicago: University of Chicago Press, 1994).

Selected Bibliography

Works cited in the text and notes that pertain to cooking or the history of food and dining.

Accademia Italiana della Cucina, *La Cucina: The Regional Cooking of Italy*. Italian title: *La Cucina del Bel Paese*. Translated by Jay Hyams. New York: Rizzoli, 2009.

Adimari, Fiamma Niccolini, and Fosco Provvedi. *Il libro d'oro dei primi piatti italiani con 1000 ricette*. Milan: Mursia, 1980.

Antolini, Piero and The Lian Tjo, *The Great Book of Chinese Cooking*. New York: International Culinary Society, 1990.

Apicius. *Apicius: Cookery and Dining in Imperial Rome*. Translated by Joseph Dommers Vehling. New York: Dover, 1977.

Artusi, Pellegrino. *Science in the Kitchen and the Art of Eating Well*. Translated by Murtha Baca and Stephen Sartarelli. Toronto: University of Toronto Press, 2003.

——. *La scienza in cucina e l'arte di mangiar bene*. Florence: Marzocco, 1960.

Athenaeus. *The Learned Banqueters*. Translated by S. Douglas Olson, 7 vols. Cambridge: Harvard University Press, 2006.

Batmanglij, Najmieh Khalili. *New Food of Life: Ancient Persian and Modern Iranian Cooking and Ceremonies*. Washington, D.C.: Mage Publishers, 2000.

Brillat-Savarin, Jean-Anthelme. *The Physiology of Taste*. Translated by Anne Drayton. New York: Penguin, 1994.

Bugialli, Giuliano. *Bugialli on Pasta*. New York: Simon and Schuster, 1988.

——. *The Fine Art of Italian Cooking*. New York: Quadrangle, 1977.

——. *The Fine Art of Italian Cooking: The Classic Cookbook, Updated and Expanded.* New York: Gramercy, 2005; orig. pub. 1977.

——. *Foods of Italy.* New York: Stewart, Tabori and Chang, 1984.

——. *Foods of Tuscany.* New York: Stewart, Tabori and Chang, 1992.

Carcopino, Jérôme. *Daily Life in Ancient Rome.* Translated by E. O. Lorimer. New Haven: Yale University Press, 1940.

Carluccio, Antonio. *A Taste of Italy.* Boston: Little Brown, 1986.

Charles, Dora. *A Real Southern Cook in Her Savannah Kitchen.* New York: Houghton Mifflin Harcourt, 2015.

Chen, Joyce. *Joyce Chen Cookbook.* Philadelphia: Lippincott, 1962.

Child, Julia. *Mastering the Art of French Cooking.* Vols. 1 and 2. New York: Knopf, 1961 and 1970.

Collin, Rima, and Richard Collin. *The New Orleans Cookbook: Creole, Cajun, and Louisiana French Recipes Past and Present.* New York: Knopf, 1977.

Dupree, Nathalie. *New Southern Cooking.* New York: Knopf, 1991.

Faas, Patrick. *Around the Roman Table.* Translated by Shaun Whiteside. Chicago: University of Chicago Press, 1994.

Gabilondo, Aída. *Mexican Family Cooking.* New York: Fawcett Columbine, 1986.

Giacosa, Ilaria Gozzini. *A Taste of Ancient Rome.* Translated by Anna Herklotz. Chicago: University of Chicago Press, 1992.

Hazan, Marcella. *Essentials of Classic Italian Cooking.* New York: Knopf, 1993.

——. *Marcella Cucina.* New York: Harper Collins, 1977.

——. *Marcella's Italian Kitchen.* New York: Knopf, 1986.

——. *Marcella Says . . .* New York: Harper Collins, 2004.

Hazan, Marcella, and Victor Hazan, *Ingredienti.* New York: Scribner, 2016.

Herbst, Sharon Tyler. *Food Lover's Companion: Comprehensive Definitions of Nearly 6000 Food, Drink, and Culinary Terms*, 3d ed. Hauppange, NY: Barron's, 2001.

The Horizon Cookbook and Illustrated History of Eating and Drinking through the Ages. Edited by Wendy Buehr. 2 vols. New York: American Heritage and Doubleday, 1968.

Kasper, Lynne Rossetto. *The Splendid Table: Recipes from Emilia-Romagna, The Heartland of Northern Italian Food*. New York: William Morrow, 1992.

Kass, Leon R. *The Hungry Soul: Eating and the Perfecting of Our Nature*. Chicago: University of Chicago Press, 1994.

Lévi-Strauss, Claude. *The Raw and the Cooked: Introduction to a Science of Mythology*. Translated by John Weightman and Doreen Weightman. New York: Harper, 1969.

Lewis, Edna and Scott Peacock. *The Gift of Southern Cooking*. New York: Knopf, 2003.

Martin, Damiano. *The da Fiori Cookbook: Recipes from Venice's Best Restaurant*. New York: William Morrow, 2003.

Montagné, Prosper. *Larousse Gastranomique*. Translated by Nina Froud, et al. New York: Crown, 1961.

Paoli, Ugo Enrico. *Vita romana*. Florence: Le Monnier, 1958.

Petroni, Paolo. *Il libro della vera cucina fiorentina: 230 ricette*. Florence: Bonechi, 1974.

Petronius. *Satyricon*. Translated by Michael Heseltine and W. H. D. Rouse. Revised by E. H. Warmington. Cambridge: Harvard University Press, 1997.

Plutarch. "The Dinner of the Seven Wise Men." In vol. 2 of *Moralia*, 346–449. Translated by Frank Cole Babbitt. Cambridge: Harvard University Press, 2002.

Prudhomme, Paul. *Chef Paul Prudhomme's Louisiana Kitchen*. New York: William Morrow, 1964.

Redon, Odile, Françoise Sabban, and Silvano Serrenti. *The Medieval Kitchen: Recipes from France and Italy*.

Translated by Edward Schneider. Chicago: University of Chicago Press, 1998.

Riley, Gillian. *The Oxford Companion to Italian Food.* New York: Oxford University Press, 2007.

———. *Renaissance Recipes.* San Francisco: Pomegranate Artbooks, 1993.

Schott, Ben. *Schott's Food and Drink Miscellany.* New York: Bloomsbury, 2004.

Scicolone, Michele. *The Antipasto Table.* New York: William Morrow, 1991.

———. *A Fresh Taste of Italy: 250 Authentic Recipes, Undiscovered Dishes, and New Flavors for Every Day.* New York: Broadway Books, 1997.

———. *1000 Italian Recipes.* New York: Wiley, 2004.

Segan, Francine. *The Philosopher's Kitchen.* New York: Random House, 2004.

The Silver Spoon. Italian title: *Il cucchiaio d'argento.* New York: Phaidon, 2005.

Verene, Donald Phillip. "Vico and Culinary Art: 'On the Sumptuous Dinners of the Romans' and the Science of the First Meals." *New Vico Studies* 20(2002): 69–78.

Vico, Giambattista. "On the Sumptuous Dinners of the Romans." Translated by George A. Trone. *New Vico Studies* 20 (2002): 79–89.

Wilson, Justin. *The Justin Wilson Gourmet and Gourmand Cookbook.* Gretna, LA: Pelican, 1989).

Zane, Eva. *Greek Cooking for the Gods.* San Francisco: 101 Productions, 1974.

Index

ibidem-Verlag / *ibidem* Press
Melchiorstr. 15
70439 Stuttgart
Germany

ibidem@ibidem.eu
ibidem.eu